KEEP COMING BACK

HARPER/HAZELDEN BOOKS OF RELATED INTEREST

KEEP COMING BACK

*The Spiritual Journey
of Recovery in
Overeaters Anonymous*

ELISABETH L.

1817

A Harper/Hazelden Book

Harper & Row, Publishers, San Francisco

New York, Cambridge, Philadelphia, St. Louis
London, Singapore, Sydney, Tokyo, Toronto

FIRST HARPER & ROW EDITION PUBLISHED IN 1989.

Library of Congress Cataloging-in-Publication Data

L., Elisabeth.
  Keep coming back.

  "A Harper/Hazelden book."
  Bibliography: p.
  Includes index.
  1. Eating disorders—Popular works. I. Title.
RC552.E18L19   1989   616.85′2   88-45661
ISBN 0-06-255497-2 (pbk.)

  90 91 92 93 MUR 10 9 8 7 6 5 4 3 2

Contents

The stories of people used in this book are not based on any person's experience but are drawn from composite experiences of many compulsive eaters.

Introduction

Maybe someday there will be a magical cure for eating disorders. Maybe a vaccine will be developed guaranteeing immunity against any urge to overeat. Maybe there will be a willpower pill to ward off binges. Maybe a magic potion will restore a normal appetite to someone who is undereating. Take two tablets at bedtime and wake up at your ideal weight! One capsule three times a day and you will eat exactly what you should—no more, no less. Maybe cows will fly.

Until that magic day arrives, what do we do? Many of us overeaters try every diet we see in print, hear about, or dream up by ourselves. We join exercise clubs, health spas, and aerobics classes. We fast, consume only liquids, and bribe ourselves with promises of new clothes when the extra pounds are shed. Some of us resort to self-induced vomiting or laxative abuse as a desperate means of weight control. Some of us weigh 350 pounds. Some of us keep dieting until we weigh 75 pounds, and still feel fat. The common thread running through the fabric of eating disorders is an obsession with food—either eating it or not eating it. The food obsession threatens to take over our lives, and we search for a way to be free of it so we will not be destroyed.

Those of us who are lucky find help. It can come from many sources, including doctors, friends, therapists, family members, nutritionists, and physical fitness experts. Some of us find our major source of help through an emotional, spiritual, and physical program of recovery—the Twelve Steps of Overeaters Anonymous.

Keep Coming Back

Recovery is not magic. It's hard work. It is ups and downs—two steps forward and one step backward. And if we're still looking for a fairy godmother with a magic wand, we're going to be disappointed.

Recovery from an eating disorder means more than simply losing or gaining pounds to maintain a healthy weight. We've all played the diet game with varying success. Though recovery certainly includes maintaining weight within a normal range, it promises much, much more. We want to restore food to its proper place in our lives so that we are eating to nourish our bodies instead of trying to use food as an all-purpose problem-solver. We want to be free of the obsession with food and diets and eating and not eating so we can discover what else is important to us. We want to live full, abundant lives, to act spontaneously instead of being trapped in compulsive behavior.

Those of us who are overeaters and bingers operate under two major delusions: (1) if we feel troubled, food will make us feel better; and (2) if we can only control our compulsion to overeat we will live happily ever after.

Some fairy tales end with the princess marrying the prince. All problems have been solved, and life from then on is a garden of roses. Real rose gardens, however, contain bugs and thorns and weeds as well as flowers, and roses need rain as much as sunshine. We also know that finding the prince or princess is only the beginning! Living with him or her is where the fairy tale leaves off and real life begins.

So it is with an eating disorder. Finding a recovery program and progressing toward a weight goal is just the beginning. Even when we achieve a weight goal, we are still just beginning. We are beginning to live the rest of our lives, one day at a time, without using food to solve problems that food cannot solve. We are beginning to deal with all of the bugs, thorns, and other issues that we ignored or buried during our binges.

The Twelve Step program of recovery is a program for living, whether we are recovering from alcoholism, other drug abuse, compulsive gambling, or food abuse. We are given a support network, new hope, and new faith. We may be strict in following the guidelines we receive, or we may be more flexible as we adapt the program to our own needs, taking what we can use and leaving the rest, perhaps for another day.

The Twelve Step program suggests we "keep coming back." Unless that fairy godmother comes along with her magic wand, we're not going to learn it all in a day, a week, a year, or even in a lifetime! Some of us will have relapses; some of us will go off on periodic searches for an easier, softer way; all of us will have problems. Recovery is not a bed of roses but a way of learning how to deal constructively with life's ups and downs without trying to escape by some quick fix.

As I see it, our options are threefold: We can give up and let our eating disorder take over and destroy our lives; we can continue to search for the magic elixir that will cure us overnight; or we can keep coming back to a program that promises emotional and spiritual growth through a Power greater than ourselves. I invite you to choose the third option. I've been doing it for twelve years, and I recommend it wholeheartedly. It's not magic, but it works.

CHAPTER ONE

Is There Life After Abstinence?

When I first heard about abstinence at an Overeaters Anonymous meeting, it sounded horrible. I was desperate, but not desperate enough. The way I heard it, abstinence was not eating sugar or refined carbohydrates and not eating between meals. Sugar and refined carbohydrates and eating between meals were what I thought made my world bearable. Yet, in some corner of my awareness I knew this was the answer. I wasn't ready for it, but I knew it was there if I really needed it. In the meantime, I would continue as a professional dieter.

That was back in the early seventies. I had been a professional dieter since I was twelve, for almost a quarter of a century. I was trying to solve the problem of not fitting into my clothes.

I had other problems, too, such as not being able to stop eating once I got started. There were also problems of not feeling like going to work, or getting dinner for my family, or having sex with my husband, or responding decently to anyone who had the misfortune of crossing my path. Other problems included feeling sick to my stomach and suddenly looking six months pregnant. My solution was temporary at best: take some Alka-Seltzer and a few laxatives and diet rigorously for several days until the next binge. But I binged more than I dieted, so the pounds kept creeping on.

My main goal in life was to wear a size eight. (I am five feet, seven-and-a-half inches tall.) It seemed to me that fitting into a size eight would guarantee a happily-ever-after existence. If I were thin, like the models I saw in magazines, life would be a dream.

Keep Coming Back

I tried all the diets (you probably know them too) and everything else that might lead to the size eight. Once in a great while I would get there for a few days or even weeks. But then several major binges would push the eights to the rear of my closet, and I would be back into bigger and bigger sizes. So when I read about Overeaters Anonymous, I decided to try that.

When I attended that first O.A. meeting, I was so focused on food that I filtered out nearly everything I heard that wasn't food-related. I do remember we ended the meeting by standing in a circle, holding hands, and saying the Lord's Prayer. That felt awkward, but it reached the part of me that knew there was an answer to my problem. People were friendly and I was invited to return, but it was years before I did.

If I could have found an easier way to stop self-destructing with food, I probably would never have returned to O.A. I searched very hard and tried many methods, but I couldn't find a satisfactory way to stop bingeing. Many of the ways I tried worked briefly—the expensive exercise club, another one of the latest diets, a new hobby—but not for long. The binges got worse, and I was scared.

Once or twice a year for about four years, I would read the O.A. literature I had received at my first meeting. Then I would sigh, return the literature to my drawer, and look for another new diet, another new interest, or a different exercise program. Toward summer's end in 1976, I had outgrown practically all of the clothes in my closet, even the big sizes. I was desperate enough to entertain the notion that abstinence was probably my only chance to stop bingeing. I was ready to hear more about it.

When I returned to O.A. and listened again, I heard about more than not overeating. I heard about making telephone calls, talking about problems, asking for help, and working a spiritual program. I heard stories from people like me who had stopped eating compulsively and found new ways to deal with life. These people told me I could do it too.

The next day I took a deep breath and decided to try this thing called abstinence. It was try or die. I wrote a food plan for the next day. Then I took several more deep breaths, and I called a woman who had told her story at the meeting, asking her if she would be my sponsor. She said yes.

The next morning I began my first day of abstinence. It was not as hard as I had expected. When I woke up the following morning, I could feel a new, inner bouyancy and hope. Even so, the idea of permanently existing without succumbing to an orgy of wallowing in my favorite foods was too frightening to contemplate. What would I do when the going got rough? I decided to follow instructions and try to take things one day at a time.

What happens after we make a commitment to abstinence? What happens when one day becomes a week, the weeks become a month, and the months become years? What happens if we slip?

What changes come about with abstinence? How does it affect our relationships with other people, our social activities, jobs, and daily routines? What do we have to adjust, give up, rearrange? What do we lose? What do we gain? How do we survive?

What happens when a few 24 hours have passed and the glow begins to fade? What do we do when abstinence stops being frightening, is no longer a challenge, and seems stale and boring?

What happens when the honeymoon ends and we return to bingeing and regain the lost pounds, plus a few more?

Abstinence: An Adventure

For me, abstinence began as a desperate remedy for a desperate problem. It was certainly a challenge, and it was definitely a chore. It was also an adventure, since I had no idea where abstinence would lead or if I would be able to follow.

At first, I concentrated on the mechanics of writing a food plan, calling it in to my sponsor, making sure I had the necessary food supplies, and trying to organize the rest of my daily routine to support the new venture.

I was lucky. My sponsor assured me each morning that I could do it. Slowly, the abstinent days began to accumulate. The discipline of eating three meals a day was a new experience. Prior to this, my latest attempt to control what I ate consisted of not eating anything for as long as possible each day—usually until about four or five in the afternoon. Then I would have a little of this and that until the little bits escalated into an enormous binge. For at least a year, I hadn't managed to stay on any structured diet for more than three days. Being able to follow a food plan was a major miracle.

I was elated as the excess pounds began to disappear. Every morning I would rise with energy and enthusiasm. But the newfound discipline felt uncertain and in danger of sliding away at any moment.

My food plan was strict. This was back when O.A. had a suggested plan known as "the grey sheet." No refined sugar or refined carbohydrates. Giving up sugar and white flour was a drastic move for me, but with some physical withdrawal and discomfort my body adjusted to the change. Sugar had been my "drug of choice" for as long as I could remember. When I stopped using it, I had headaches and cravings and crying spells, but after about three days the headaches were gone, the crying spells less frequent, and the cravings less intense.

I tried to "keep it simple." During the first week, for dinner every night I had two hot dogs (no buns) with mustard, a vegetable, and a salad. Hot dogs were never one of my binge foods, so I figured they were safe. I would fix a big salad in the morning when my resistance was high, so I would be less tempted to nibble during preparation. I would also go to the grocery store in the morning when the cravings were quieter. Since late afternoons and evenings had always been my downfall, I tried to stay out of the kitchen at those times.

So far, abstinence might sound dull and like another of those latest diets. "So where's the reward?" you ask. Well, for one thing, I felt like getting up in the morning and moving vigorously into the day's activities. Before abstinence, I would be so hung over from the previous evening's binge that any activity was a huge hurdle to be avoided if possible.

What made abstinence an adventure for me was that I was doing it one day at a time, one meal at a time. Diets have beginnings and endings, often too many of both! For most of us, the endings usually come prematurely, before we accomplished what we set out to do. Abstinence is not a diet. It is a way of life.

I still may contemplate eating another dish (or half gallon) of ice cream. But I can, for instance, choose not to eat ice cream today. And I can choose to abstain again tomorrow. I am free to make a choice. I am not locked into the tyranny of either a diet or a binge.

Before many weeks had passed, I discovered I could not maintain my abstinence and consume alcohol. Not drinking at parties was very uncomfortable at first, since alcohol had activated my social self for many years. Because I felt awkward and exposed without drinking, I avoided social situations whenever possible for about a year.

That was okay. I allowed myself to be antisocial for a while. Since food was also a problem for me at parties, one of the adjustments I made was to eliminate unappealing social events. When I did go to a party, I went to be with the people, not for the food and drink. It was an adventure to learn to survive and enjoy myself without abandoning my food plan. Eventually I enjoyed myself much more, since I was more fully present.

A common definition of abstinence in O.A. is, "three moderate meals a day with nothing in between and no binge foods." What seemed severe self-denial was becoming a road to greater fun and freedom.

Once I was eating only three meals a day, I no longer needed to be continually close to the kitchen. What would I do with the rest of my life? How would I spend the time I had formerly spent eating? I had not worked full time in the outside world for years. Could I, at age 39, find some interesting and useful job? Could I manage working 8 hours daily outside my home? Would I be able to make it out there, away from the so-called safety of my kitchen? The possibilities were exciting, and at the same time, fearsome.

Yes, I was afraid, but along with abstinence I had more courage. Why not get career counseling? Why not talk to my husband's business friends and see if I might fit in somewhere? Frightening? Yes. An adventure? Definitely.

Abstinence: Invitation to Intimacy

When I was bingeing, food was my primary source of comfort, joy, courage, compensation, and celebration. Eating was my vehicle for expressing anger, hurt, sadness, happiness, and longing. Since early adolescence I had been involved in a long-term love affair with cake, cookies, ice cream, and Danish pastry. Instead of talking about my problems, I ate.

Then came abstinence. Calling my sponsor to give her my food plan. Discussing with her the difficulties I was having. Talking about my problems instead of eating. Going to meetings. Hearing about other people's problems. Disclosing my inner turmoil. Feeling that I was in a safe place with people who understood and accepted me. Sharing hurts, angers, and embarrassments that I had kept under tight wraps for decades.

My O.A. friends were safe to talk to, and it was a tremendous relief to find people who knew what I was talking about. But what about the rest of the world? What about my other friends? What about my family?

I grew up thinking I should be able to solve my problems without help, and that I shouldn't reveal much about how I was feeling, because I would be vulnerable and exposed. I smiled, I was a "good girl," a "good sport." If I was angry, I would try not to show it, because nice, charming girls didn't get mad. If I had warm, loving feelings toward someone, I didn't express them, because I felt the person might reject me.

I used food to keep a lid on my feelings. My relationships with others may have been shallow, but that seemed safer.

When we stop using food to try to fill emotional needs, we have to find a new method of getting those needs met. New hungers begin to surface and one of these hungers is for intimacy with others—physical intimacy, emotional intimacy, and spiritual intimacy.

I began on the path toward intimacy when I called my O. A. friends on the telephone, talked with them at meetings, and began listening to them. I saw I could talk to someone about being mad at my husband instead of dealing with the emotion by eating an entire box of crackers. That change came relatively easily. What was harder and more risky was expressing my anger to my husband constructively so that, together, we could work on the problem and reach a deeper intimacy. Just admitting that I needed him and that bingeing was not a satisfactory substitute was hard to do.

Being abstinent meant I would have to depend on other people. I couldn't maintain the pretense of "going it alone." Being abstinent meant I would have to examine my relationships and determine how healthy they were. I was changing, and that change would affect everyone around me. What would be the outcome?

There was no way I could be abstinent without being honest, not only about food, but also about my feelings. Honesty brings genuine intimacy, cutting through our webs of indifference.

Without too much food, my emotions rose more quickly to the surface. I began to say "ouch" when something hurt, first only to myself, but gradually out loud. I allowed myself to feel regret and remorse when I had done the hurting, and I got brave enough to say, "I'm sorry." Slowly I learned to say "I love you" to family members and friends without being embarrassed.

Intimacy doesn't mean lack of conflict. A superficial relationship can sail along smoothly, since deep feelings are not involved. When we truly care about someone, however, we are open to hurt, anger, and disappointment. If we cannot or will not express these feelings, then the relationship does not evolve to deeper intimacy.

Coming close to others is risky, especially for those of us who have spent so much of our lives using food to try to satisfy our emotional needs. When I was overweight, I felt unattractive, unloveable, and uninteresting. Who could possibly want to know the real me? And who was "the real me" anyway? There was no way I could find that person alone. Discovering who I was could only be done by telling other people how I felt, what I thought, my fantasies, fears, and hopes. Scary!

Would life after abstinence leave my tender feelings bruised? Would my anger destroy certain precarious relationships? Would my marriage survive? Would my children suffer? Would I leap into other compulsive behaviors as substitutes for food binges?

One thing was sure. Some changes would be made. If ice cream and cookies were no longer the mainstays of my support network, then some live hearts and bodies were going to be required. I would accept the invitation to intimacy, knowing there would be pain as well as pleasure.

Abstinence: A Spiritual Journey

Abstinence was bringing changes. I was eating three moderate meals a day and not bingeing. I was losing extra pounds and feeling better. I was turning to people instead of food to satisfy my emotional hungers. I was learning to recognize and express my feelings.

Something else was happening. Slowly, I was coming to depend on a Power greater than myself to manage my life. I knew that for abstinence to work for me, it had to be different from the diets I had tried in the past. Somehow I had to get the strength to stay with it and not give up, as I had done so many times before.

Initially, I wasn't much interested in the Twelve Steps,* because my goal was a size eight. I was ready, however, to take Step One, since it was very clear that I was "powerless over food" and that my life "had become unmanageable." With that First Step, my spiritual journey began.

The other Steps followed as I saw there was no way to maintain abstinence by myself. Strength had to come from somewhere else. That "somewhere else" was the power of the group—the fellowship—and the Higher Power I choose to call God.

"I'm depending on you, God," was what I said first thing in the morning and often during the day. Before abstinence, I functioned as though food were my Higher Power. It was what I turned to in times of stress, sadness, joy, anxiety, fear, boredom, and frustration.

I believe the most significant promise of life after abstinence is the potential for spiritual growth. By depending on a Higher Power, rather than food, for an emotional uplift, the possibilities for healthy changes are limitless. However, spiritual journeys don't necessarily follow a straight line.

When I started my progression through the Twelve Steps, I expected an orderly journey from one to the next. Instead, I frequently backtracked. It was amazing how easily I could forget that I was powerless over food! Back to Step One. I would decide to let God be in charge of my will and my life at seven in the morning, and an hour later I would be tied in knots trying to run the show my way. Back to Step Three.

When I started the journey, I didn't expect to get through all Twelve Steps. I believed that twelve might be necessary for some, but I was different. I would get to that size eight much more quickly, without all that hassle.

---

* The Twelve Steps of Overeaters Anonymous are reprinted at the end of the book.

Sure I would—when cows could fly and when fairy god-mothers came around waving wands.

I liked Steps One, Two, Three, Eleven, and Twelve. My preference would have been to omit those other seven Steps. But others in O.A. and my sponsor told me that skipping Steps I didn't like might not be a good idea, and they were right. After a few unsuccessful experiments with my abridged version of the program, I concluded that to maintain abstinence, it would be wise to follow directions carefully and take all of the Steps.

Spiritual journeys take time. I began reading a daily meditation book for pre-breakfast nourishment. After a while, I discovered I could go back to that book at difficult times during the day. Writing helped, as did sitting still and letting "conscious contact" with the God of my understanding occur.

What happens when we give up the idea of trying to control our lives (and very possibly the lives of others too) and decide to let a Higher Power take over? I felt I was taking a huge risk. How would I know if there really is a Higher Power? And even if there is, what assurance was there that I would be taken care of?

It was a leap into the unknown, but that leap seemed more attractive than staying mired in my old misery. Things were not going well, so what did I have to lose? I saw this new way working for other people. Also, I had a dim memory of a time when faith in God made my world secure.

For some of us, the concept of spirituality may seem unreal. We may think living spiritually means becoming preoccupied with visions of some vague, mystical hereafter, rather than living in the here and now.

My experience is just the opposite. I find the more I concentrate on my spiritual journey, the more present I am in the real events of each moment. For me, overeating is an escape from reality into a private world of fantasy. Being abstinent makes me aware of what is really going on.

Tuning in to the spiritual reality of now prevents me from getting stuck in regrets or resentments of the past. I can let go of them. I can also avoid worrying about the future, since that is God's department. I can focus on the present.

When I first heard about abstinence, I feared it would wipe out my pleasures and threaten my ability to cope. Instead I found new pleasures and new ways of coping.

Abstinence was setting me free to function in the present and to be aware of my spiritual journey. I was escaping from a prison-world of fantasy and compulsion into the world of reality. The Twelve Steps were pointing the way—O. A. members in the meeting rooms were helping, and gradually "the" program was becoming "my" program.

CHAPTER TWO

Where's The Finish Line?

I was working the program, and the program was working for me. Some slipping and sliding occurred during that first year, but I was on track. I knew where I wanted to go: to a binge-free life in a size eight. And I knew how to get there: by abstinence and the Twelve Steps. My honeymoon in the program lasted for about twelve months. During that time, I focused on maintaining my abstinence, attending meetings, and working the Steps. Important decisions about major changes in my life were postponed.

After a year in the program, I wore a size eight and I had gone through all Twelve Steps. So I graduated and lived happily ever after, right?

Wrong.

After Size Eight, Then What?

Making my way through the big sizes in my closet down to the eights was a wonderful trip. Despite a few minor detours and temporary roadblocks, there was no doubt where I was headed—to the mecca of slenderness, a never-never-land where all of my problems would be solved because I would at last be glamorous, attractive, and youthful-looking.

When I reached my destination, however, the few size eights I had collected over the years during my fleeting thin periods had gone out of style. That was fine, since part of the fun was getting new clothes. I became a professional shopper. Since I had more time than money, I searched avidly for bargains in discount stores, used-clothing shops, and on the sale racks of department stores and boutiques. I bought patterns and material, took out my sewing machine, and covered the dining room table with pieces of new outfits, along with larger clothes from my closet that I decided to alter.

I loved looking at myself in the fitting room mirrors and seeing streamlined curves where ugly, fatty rolls and bulges once protruded. I loved the compliments from friends and the admiring glances of strangers. My husband was delighted.

I felt energetic in a size eight. I took long walks on the beach, even breaking into a slow jog now and then. My children were amazed. My new energy, however, didn't come from the size eights; it came from being abstinent and not bogged down with extra calories. Even more important, the energy came from being tuned in to a Higher Power.

Before abstinence, I could easily have kept moving on up the line, from size eight to size ten, then twelve, then fourteen. But I would manage to shove myself into reverse and start back down, temporarily at least. Food and eating, diets and binges were my obsession. This allowed me to ignore other troublesome parts of my life, such as messy closets, marital problems, career concerns, and unhappy adolescents.

This time, with help from my Higher Power, I was determined to stay off the up-and-down, binge-diet seesaw so I could begin to deal with the other issues. I was willing to go to any lengths to keep from moving back up the scale. I was briefly tempted to continue going down: If size eight was great, wouldn't size six be even better? I could keep losing pounds and have the thrill of seeing the scale indicator moving down when I weighed myself each month.

One deterrent to accomplishing a size six was that I was tired of altering clothes. Another was that I couldn't afford to buy a new wardrobe. The most powerful deterrent, however, was provided by a speaker at an O.A. meeting. This speaker had weighed over 200 pounds when she was 32. Two years later she was down to 75 pounds and was hospitalized for anorexia. When I heard her, three years beyond that low point, she was working the program and maintaining a normal weight.

She described her compulsion to get thinner and thinner, and I understood exactly. After size six, then what? Size four? Size two? Tube feedings? No thanks.

I hoped my progression through sizes, either up or down, was over. Simply maintaining size eight would be fantastic progress. The key to doing it was in "keep coming back," as this woman had suggested, and in "working the Steps."

After Step Twelve, Then What?

As I said earlier, I liked Steps One, Two, and Three. I was ready to let God take over, in spite of some recurring doubts. As for Step Four, I had avoided taking inventory as long as possible, but about halfway through my first year in the program I was having trouble with abstinence. Since most anything was preferable to losing that, I began work on a Fourth Step inventory.

The inventory was to be shared with another person. Whom would I choose? Finding a perfect stranger appealed to me. Maybe I could get on an airplane or a Greyhound bus and sit beside a sympathetic-looking person whom I would never see again. That seemed the easiest way of divulging my dark and embarrassing secrets.

But I abandoned that idea and decided to go to the minister of our family church. Calling the minister, and explaining why I wanted to see him, was perhaps even more risky than the first time I called my sponsor and asked for her help. I was moving outside the Twelve-Step family to someone who might not understand.

I'm not sure whether he understood. Getting to his office and beginning the inventory was an ordeal. I nervously read the four pages, not trusting myself to speak extemporaneously. I don't remember much about the minister's response, except that his comments were supportive rather than critical. I walked out the church door feeling a wonderful sense of relief. I had done it! Some very grimy corners of my past had been exposed to the light and, like shadows, they had vanished. What had seemed so dark and dreadful became amazingly lighter when revealed to another person.

After giving my inventory, I was faced with five remaining Steps. Six and Seven—being ready for God to remove my character defects and humbly asking Him to remove my shortcomings—did not present insurmountable problems. I wasn't big on humility, but I was ready to be rid of my character defects. Step Ten—continuous personal inventory—did not loom too large, since I was already doing a daily review before going to bed, and I was becoming more prompt and sincere about admitting when I was wrong. The hang-up was with Steps Eight and Nine, dealing with making a list and making amends.

Whom had I harmed, and how was I going to make amends? I delayed serious consideration of Steps Eight and Nine for months. Then one night I sat down and made a list, which was relatively painless to do. The list consisted of half a dozen people. I'm sure I had hurt others, but the major damage had been done to the six individuals closest to me.

Making amends included writing letters, talking face-to-face with others, and especially focusing on ways to change my old behavior and improve present relationships. I believed the best amend I could make to the people I loved was to maintain my abstinence so I would be emotionally available to them. Maintaining abstinence was also the best amend I could make to myself for the harm done by my compulsive bingeing and dieting.

Central to the amends process for me was staying in contact with a Higher Power. That was the only way I could let go of pride and self-will long enough to apologize for my mistakes and try to correct them.

When I reached Step Ten, I began to realize that the Twelve Steps weren't a temporary diversion, but a continuing process. It would be nice if we could each take twelve steps and then a couple of hops and suddenly find ourselves soaring off in flight, but we know the program doesn't work that way.

I thought maybe some day I would reach a point where the Twelve Steps would be so ingrained I could forget about them and travel on automatic pilot. But then, there were still days when I couldn't even remember Step One!

After the New Job, Then What?

So after a year in the program, I wore a size eight and had at least a passing acquaintance with each of the Twelve Steps. What about the rest of my life? Wasn't it time to start thinking about things like who did I want to spend my life with? How was I going to have the food, clothing, and shelter I needed if I parted from my husband? And what should I do with my time and talents?

I had been married for seventeen years. My children were fifteen and twelve. For about five years I had taught piano at home. It helped me make a little money and still be around when my son and daughter returned from school in the afternoons. Teaching piano was not something I loved to do, and the time was not far off when I would be the only one home after school. Increasingly, my children were becoming involved in their own activities.

What did I want to be when I grew up? I was 40, and I still didn't know. I did know I wanted to make enough money to finance my children's college education. And I had fantasies of becoming able to support myself so that when and if the time seemed right and I had enough guts, I could consider moving away from a marriage that was more dead than alive.

Pretty scary stuff to contemplate. Before abstinence, when thinking about money for college, getting a job, and leaving the marriage, I'd get so frightened I'd immediately run to the refrigerator and eat away the terrifying anxiety. Then I was so busy feeling guilty and sick, hating myself, and obsessing about food and diets that there was no time or energy left for the real issues. I buried my head in binges so I wouldn't see these issues or have to deal with them.

Keep Coming Back

After abstinence, the issues were in plain view, and I could no longer put off facing them. The most pressing problem was finding a job, which raised the question of, what did I want to do with the rest of my life? What appealed to me most was the idea of being a freelance writer. In 1975 I had taken a correspondence course on writing for children and had spent many morning hours at my typewriter composing what I thought were charming and saleable stories. I sent them to magazine editors and book publishers, and a few weeks or months later I'd find the stories back in my mailbox with rejection slips.

All indications were that no one could begin to make it through college on the proceeds of my writing. I did manage to sell a poem, but the check I received from the *Christian Science Monitor* was barely enough to cover one college application fee. Clearly, I needed help. I put away my typewriter and signed up for a career counseling program.

After a series of tests and several weeks of group and individual counseling sessions, my sights were set toward merchandising women's clothing. My ambition then was to become a buyer for a women's specialty store. Think of all the size eights I could obtain at discount prices! Back from retirement came the typewriter just long enough to roll out a fresh resume, and I was ready to hit the pavement and market myself.

But I was apprehensive. Fear made me want to turn around and head back to the comfort and security of my kitchen, but I knew what I would find there was false security and more pain. Could I handle the job hunt challenge? My sponsor said I could do it. The O.A. members in the meeting rooms said I could do it. My family and friends said I could do it.

On the Monday after Thanksgiving 1978, I began working full time in a large department store's china and crystal section. What happened to women's fashions? That was going to come later, I thought. First I would get some general training. After Christmas I moved to linens, and soon I began looking for another job.

Before abstinence, I probably would have stayed with the job out of inertia and fear of change, in spite of quickly realizing that it wasn't what I wanted. And I would have tried to binge away my frustration. This time, however, I went to an employment agency and got a job as secretary to the executive director of a national association. In six months I was ready to move again, and found a group of trade associations that needed an administrative assistant. Six months later, a friend told me about a job that involved writing and editing and required a background in music. I was not looking for a new job at the time, but this was a marvelous opportunity and I applied. I was hired and stayed there for almost four years.

So after the new job came another, and another, and another. Where's the finish line?

When Is It Over?

Size eight, Twelve Steps, and a series of new jobs. Wasn't it time now for the graduation ceremony? I was wearing the same clothes from one year to the next, and I was out in the working world producing a steady income. Everyone was saying how good I looked. I was accomplishing things. Why did I still feel a deep emptiness inside? When could I stop spending time and energy on food plans and sponsors and Steps and meetings? When could I just relax and enjoy life?

I was very tempted, now that I wore a size eight, to try an occasional indulgence. All the rest of my life without chocolate ice cream? Without a Scotch and soda before dinner? Then I would remember that all I had to worry about was today, one day at a time—never mind the rest of my life.

I know some people in O.A. can handle desserts and an occasional alcoholic beverage. Specific food plans are up to the individual, because food is not the problem. Living is the problem. We each have to find what works for us individually.

As for the emptiness I felt inside, that was one of my living problems. I had proven over and over that no amount of food would fill the inner emptiness. Through the Steps, I was getting glimpses of fullness here and there, but those glimpses didn't last. I had thought, naively, that wearing a size eight was all I needed to make me forever happy, but it wasn't enough. Neither were the new jobs.

Is this all there is? I found myself wondering. Well, there were still the Steps, which would never be finished no matter how many times I worked them. There were still meetings, where O. A. members told me to "keep coming back." And there was still my Higher Power.

CHAPTER THREE

Help, I'm Stuck!

Experience varies in the Twelve Step programs. Some of us are lucky enough to immediately stop overeating or drinking or using other drugs or gambling or whatever. Others need more time, going to many meetings before being able to find abstinence. Some find it quickly and then lose it. Some are on and off abstinence continually. Some don't find abstinence, and leave the program. Some find it, lose it, leave, and come back.

My experience has included many "off abstinence" periods. I have never stopped trying—the goal is there each morning—but weeks have passed without one completely abstinent day. When I'm being generous with myself, I call these periods "sloppy abstinence." When I'm being tough, I say I've lost it. I like to believe that even when my abstinence is sloppy or lost, I am still making progress with the program. As people have told me so often, the important thing is to keep coming back.

Throughout my first four years in the program, I kept coming back. I would backslide for brief periods, but I don't think I ever went for longer than two weeks without a meeting. I continued to read Twelve Step literature and meditate each day, even when my food plan was a fantasy rather than a reality. Although the newness of O.A. and the Twelve Steps had faded for me after the first year, I had a program that worked. There was no doubt that my life was infinitely better than it had been previously.

Then came 1980, and midway through that year something inside of me went on strike. On the surface, I was working my program, but underneath I remained empty and looking for something to fill the void. Since I had abstinence, a good job and size eight clothes that fit, I thought my former problems were solved. Why wasn't I happy? What was missing?

I was growing more and more convinced that I was married to the wrong man. I had expected to live happily ever after once I stopped bingeing and got an interesting job. Well, I was not bingeing, but I was not happy. I figured my marriage must be what was keeping me out of paradise.

Getting Married, Getting Divorced

People in O.A. told me that getting married and getting divorced are two of many ways we try to stop bingeing and control our weight. We think that if we can arrange external circumstances the right way, we won't want to overeat. Moving, changing jobs, starting school, graduating—the list of outside incentives can go on indefinitely. But sooner or later we learn that it is our response to external circumstances that troubles us, not the circumstances themselves.

Our responses to circumstances can be more easily changed than the circumstances themselves. Through the program, we learn that we are powerless over people, places, and things, as well as food.

The question is, when do we need serenity to accept what we cannot change, and when do we need courage to change what we can? As we work the Twelve Step program, we ask and pray for enough wisdom to know the difference. For me, change came, but not until 1984.

Since this is a book about the program, and not about marriage and divorce, I won't go into specific details about what broke up a twenty-three-and-a-half-year-old marriage. For four years I stewed over whether to stay or leave. By this time, I believed that I had solved my eating disorder, since my weight was okay and my job was going well. Unfortunately, I let the marriage issue take precedence over emotional and spiritual growth.

We need to continue to grow emotionally and spiritually in order to deal with everyday minor stress, as well as major crises.

All of us have times when we feel stuck and unable to get out of a bind. We can get stuck in depression, in self-defeating ways of thinking and acting, in harmful relationships, in boredom, and in unhealthy habits. When this happens, it is tempting to look to some event that we think will magically make everything better. Back to the idea of the fairy godmother and her wand, and flying cows. "When I graduate from high school . . ." "When I get a job . . ." " When I get a better job . . ." "When I get married . . ." "When I get divorced . . ." "When I move . . ." "When my children are grown . . ." "When I retire . . ."

These external changes rearrange the outside of our lives, but the inner core remains the same. That inner core is where we live, whether we're married, single, unemployed, or chairperson of the board.

When we graduate from high school or college we may continue to binge. We get jobs, we get married, move, have children, and still we binge. Some of us get divorced; our children grow up and leave home; we get better jobs and make more money. I have done all of these things; yet in times of stress, abstinence is still a problem.

Food is my drug of choice. Each day I must come to terms with eating reasonably and refrain from using excessive amounts of food as "uppers" or "downers." The only way I can do this is by giving priority to my program. For me, abstinence is eating three moderate meals a day and avoiding sugar and alcohol. Of equal or even greater importance, however, are the program's emotional and spiritual components. Working the Steps and staying in contact with my Higher Power keeps me on track. When I forget this, I get stuck.

Who Will Rescue Me?

There may be a part of us that still hopes to find an "easier, softer way." Wouldn't it be nice to find an outside rescuer, someone who will know all the answers, tell us what to do, and make our lives fun, exciting, fulfilled, and peaceful? I had those fantasies. I tried and failed to make my husband into that person.

In January of 1984 my husband and I separated, and in January of 1985 we were divorced. Fortunately, by this time I had begun to realize that whether I was married or single, in a relationship or on my own, wearing a size eight or a size twelve, there would be problems to solve. No one could magically solve them for me or make them go away. Food was not the answer. A new partner was not the answer either. I became romantically involved with a very nice man, a possible rescuer, and guess what? Some of the same issues that forced the break up of my marriage began to surface all over again. Could it be that the problems were my own? Before long, the nitty-gritty details of reality began to penetrate the rosy, romantic haze. I was stuck again.

But I was not stuck continually. I was learning to ask for help. Sharing at meetings helped to keep me emotionally together through those very difficult years. Thanks to the program, I became much more open about my problems, instead of hiding my weaknesses and vulnerability.

As a consequence, questions began to surface. How could I best function in the real world? Did I want a committed relationship with another person? Or did I want to live alone, possibly for the rest of my life? Where did my Higher Power fit in?

I hoped to get answers to these questions, and had another important and related goal. I wanted to learn how to be so comfortable with myself that if I were intimately involved with someone else, it would be because of choice rather than dependency. I felt that until I was strong enough to live comfortably by myself, I wouldn't have much to give to another person. I decided I did not need a rescuer.

Let's Talk

When I was growing up, and until recently, eating was easier than talking about what bothered me. If I was sad, angry, afraid—even joyous—I was more apt to eat than to tell someone. Although many of us in the program do a lot of talking, we all know what it's like to cover up our true feelings with food.

I learned to talk about how I felt with my O.A. sponsor and with close program friends. Sharing inner feelings with family members and significant others, however, was very difficult for me. It always had been. As an only child, I kept my cards close to my chest and was reluctant to let other people into my private world.

It is hard for people to understand and support us if we don't let them know how we feel. Because intimacy means taking the risk of revealing ourselves to those close to us, there is fear that they may not like what they see and reject us.

During my time in Twelve Step programs (in addition to O.A., I have gone to numerous A.A. and Al-Anon meetings), I have learned that the longer I wait to ask for help, the longer I am stuck. Asking for help is not the same as looking for a rescuer. I need help in finding the solution and getting unstuck.

We are apt to get stuck when we fail to recognize our inner feelings and reactions to outer events and other people. When we are not aware of our anger, we may turn it in on ourselves and become depressed. If we are afraid and try to repress the fear, we may become paralyzed and unable to act. When we don't recognize our legitimate needs and take concrete steps to satisfy them, something inside of us says, *What's the use?* Communication is crucial. Talking with other people helps us to understand where we are. We may not need advice as much as we need to be heard and affirmed. Pride often prevents us from communicating. Perhaps we don't like to admit we are hurt, upset, or bothered by what someone has done.

Being overly concerned about pleasing others keeps us from communicating how we really feel. If we are too intent on pleasing others, we do things their way and bury our own desires and needs. Sooner or later resentments will surface and undermine the relationship.

I know I am stuck when food and eating threaten to get out of control. I know I am stuck when I see daily activities as drudgery, or when I feel bored and negative. These are the times when I need to talk, first with myself and my Higher Power, and then with the people around me. There are always solutions, but we won't find them if we keep our problems bottled up inside. Whether the issue is a bad marriage or a flat tire, help is available. For me one of the great gifts of the program is a place to go and people to listen when I need to talk. Therapy, support groups, friends, family members—all help when we are willing to be open and ask for what we need.

Where Are You, Higher Power?

Ours is a program for living. We might begin thinking the problem deals with food, weight, and diets, but if we keep coming back, we see that these considerations are merely the tip of the compulsive eater's iceberg. If we stay focused on what we eat, what we weigh, and how we look, to the exclusion of emotional and spiritual growth, we get stuck.

We may also get stuck if a job or a relationship becomes the be-all and end-all of our existence. While love and work are vitally important, we will run into trouble if we allow either to become all-consuming. Giving precedence to a Higher Power is the only method I know of maintaining balance.

There are several ways we can lose contact with our Higher Power. One is to think that everything depends on our efforts. For example, I will be anxious about a new job and get caught up in compulsive work, forgetting Step Three: turning our will and our lives over to the care of God. Or I might go off on such an emotional high that I forget about needing a Higher Power. This can happen when I'm infatuated, which can be a different kind of compulsion. Another way is to get bored with spiritual exercise and let my program of prayer and meditation lapse.

My first reaction when the contact is slipping is to think God has deserted me—or that, worse yet, there isn't a Higher Power after all. When things are going well, it's easy to succumb to the delusion that I can take care of everything by myself. When things are not going well, I can simply say, "That's the way the cookie crumbles," and try to endure. When I'm really stuck and my world threatens to fall apart, I go back to Steps One and Two and become humble enough to understand that God is not lost, but I am.

When I can't seem to find my Higher Power, the danger is that I'll try to figure out how to manage alone. For me, that has not worked. There are ways to get back in touch. I can read something inspiring and meditate. I can go to a meeting. I can talk to a fellow program member who is also trying to work the Steps. I can do something for someone who needs my help. But probably the best thing I can do, and the easiest, is to find a quiet place, be still, and let my Higher Power find me.

By clearing unnecessary debris out of our lives, we make room for God. If we're too busy, too tired, too ambitious, too filled with self-will and our own concerns, little space is left for a Higher Power. And then we wonder why we're stuck and can't find solutions to our problems! Step Three: "Made a decision to turn our will and our lives over to the care of God *as we understood Him.*"

This is the way we get unstuck.

The Power that moves us gently but firmly in the right direction is always available.

CHAPTER FOUR

We Don't Stand Still

At a recent meeting, a friend was talking about how easily she forgets she is a compulsive overeater. She periodically says to herself, *I don't really need to have a food plan any longer. I'm doing fine. And I can get along without meetings. I think I can be normal now.* She described how she would put her program on the shelf, but admitted that pretending to be normal doesn't work for very long.

Often, we seem to be standing still. We've been coming to meetings for a few months, or even a few years. We've made progress with the Steps. But the newness has worn off, and the challenge has faded. If we're doing well with abstinence, we may begin to think we can relax and eat "normally." If we're not doing well, we may say, "What's the use?" and give up.

For this compulsive overeater, experience shows that the disorder does not go away. My inclination to eat far more than I need can be controlled but, as far as I know, not cured. Consequently, when I am under stress, bored, anxious, or simply in the presence of a refrigerator filled with food, my tendency is to think about eating.

Like my friend, I am frequently tempted to put my program on the shelf while I concentrate on the rest of my life, forgetting that, without my program, the rest of my life becomes unmanageable. I can recall more than a few times when my concern about love or work or something else had taken priority over my program. I, too, can easily entertain the notion that "I must be normal by now." But when I put my program on hold, the results are not good.

Standing still? We hear in the meeting rooms that we do not stand still. Life is never static; to be alive is to be in motion.

I am either making progress with the program, turning more and more of my daily activities over to the management of a Higher Power—or I am moving in the reverse direction, trying to run the show my way. Thus, when I think I'm putting my program on hold to concentrate on some particular concern, such as a new job or a new romance, what I'm really doing is going off on my own—according to my will, not God's. I am neglecting my inner voice and spiritual resources. For a while, I can run on the spiritual reserves I have built up, but I find these reserves need to be replenished regularly. Otherwise, I am in danger of again letting food (or my job, or a relationship, or something else) replace God as my Higher Power.

But I Want It Now!

How much time did you spend, without outside help, trying to take care of your eating disorder? If we could do it alone, without a program and support group, most of us probably would. Where do some of us get the idea that a few doses of the program should take care of us for life, that if we've gone to meetings for a few months or a few years and we're still having problems, the program must not work?

"Oh yes, I tried O.A. It helped for a while, but then nothing appeared to be happening. I guess I got turned off by a couple of very overweight people in my group who sat around talking about God, but didn't look as though they were getting anywhere with their problems." When I hear a comment such as this, I have some questions to ask:

- Will you let another person's apparent lack of progress be an excuse to stop working the program yourself?
- If you feel you're in a rut, how about trying another group?
- What are your alternatives to coming back—what else is there that you haven't tried?

People with diabetes cannot cure their disease, but many control it with daily doses of insulin. Likewise, we Twelve

Steppers have a treatment program that works if we apply it regularly, whether or not we think we need it. "I am a compulsive overeater, and this program is my medicine," says Bob, who has been coming back for six years.

Meetings are our lifeline. When we expose ourselves long enough and often enough to the experience, strength, and hope of other Twelve Steppers, we hear what we need to hear and we learn. Some like to say we "catch" this program from those who already have it. We may think nothing is happening, but growth is often so slow as to be nearly imperceptible.

Eating disorders rarely, if ever, disappear instantly. We live in an age of speed—fast food, instamatic cameras, jet aircraft, microwave ovens, and same-day service. So when we work the program, we might expect quick results, and when progress is slow or seems nonexistent, we become impatient.

Did you ever plant a tree? From day to day you can't see it getting bigger, but if you measure it from one season to the next you can realize its growth. Like the tree, our growth takes time. Just as knowledge is acquired slowly, new habits of thinking and acting become solid through weeks, months, and years of repetition.

The best way we can work the Twelve Step program is one day at a time. If we look at ourselves on a particular day, we may appear to be standing still. But the next time you feel you are making no progress, ask yourself the following question: Am I abstinent at this moment? If the answer is yes, then you are making progress. Put together 24 hours of such moments and you have a new kind of day to build on for the future.

Ask yourself if, during the last 24 hours, you have let go of one situation that was beyond your control. If the answer is yes, that's progress. Ask yourself if, during the past week, you can remember a time when you consciously realized you were powerless over someone else's behavior and accepted it. If so, you are making progress.

Although we can't always see our progress, regularly using the program's tools keeps us moving in the right direction.

Going to meetings, making phone calls, reading Twelve Step literature, writing about how we feel—these are things we need to do, even when we think we're standing still. Eventually, our progress will be measurable. If we get impatient with the apparent slowness and let our program slide, we may realize before long that, instead of standing still, we are going backward. Do I hear someone saying, "Yes, God. Please give me patience, and give it to me now"?

But You Look Great

"They all told me how great I looked," Jane P. says with a wry smile, "and even though I should have known I was definitely not great on the inside, I began to believe I was."

Some of us with eating disorders appear outwardly to "have it all together." Jane had been an overachieving, perfectionistic adolescent who tried to please everyone and lost herself in the process. Her mother became terminally ill with cancer when Jane was sixteen, and Jane became anorexic. Her menstrual periods stopped and her weight dropped to a dangerously low level. She didn't look as though she "had it all together" then.

After treatment for anorexia, Jane regained her normal weight, and then, when she went away to college, began to binge. As more and more pounds piled on, she became very upset. She believed, along with making straight A's and being well-liked, she should have the perfect figure. Bulimia seemed to be the solution. Jane started purging regularly—by self-induced vomiting or by taking large amounts of laxatives. On the surface, she looked fine, but she had become obsessed with food—alternately dieting, bingeing, and purging.

In a second treatment program, Jane, then 21, was introduced to O.A. Her eating disorder had forced her to drop out of school. But with therapy and O.A. she was able to return to school a year later.

"I did okay for the first few months," recalls Jane. "Then the pressures of papers and exams began to get to me. I didn't think I had time to go to meetings. I thought, after six and a half years and two treatment programs, I should be cured. I let my program go while I worked on making the Dean's List. I got more and more uptight, and the only way I could relax was to binge on something sweet. I didn't want to get back into purging, and I was terrified of being fat, so I wouldn't eat anything for a day or two after I binged. I managed not to gain weight, and my friends and family thought everything was fine.

"I told myself that once I graduated and got away from the pressure of school, I'd get back to normal eating. That didn't happen. I made the Dean's List, graduated with honors, got a fantastic job, and continued to binge and fast. I still didn't have time to go to O.A. meetings. Everyone continued to tell me how great I looked, and I decided what I was doing was okay, since I was getting away with it.

"I went on like that for three years. I got more and more uptight about my job. My social life went down to zilch, because I was either exhausted from fasting or I wanted to be alone to binge. It was when I started gaining weight and went back to purging that I finally realized I was in a real mess."

Jane had thought she was standing still when bingeing and fasting. How easy it is for other people's approval and admiration to delude us. Like Jane, we can put up such a good front that we almost fool ourselves. When we focus on pleasing the outside world, however, we do it at the price of inner peace and satisfaction. Somewhere down deep, we know things are not right. We're not facing the real issues. A poor self-image is often part of our problem—an important part. Lack of self-esteem makes us greedy for outside approval.

Being obsessed with how we look and what we weigh is part of the illness. Before O.A., some of us were weighing ourselves several times a day. The program, by contrast, suggests we weigh ourselves only once a month. If we need to lose pounds, it should be done slowly. Fluctuations can be expected, and if we need a daily or even weekly indication of weight loss to make us feel good we may become discouraged.

Our culture's emphasis on being slim and trim as the pathway to popularity and success affects many women, and men too. Fortunately, the criteria for what is attractive is showing signs of moving more toward being healthy and fit than being superthin.

Eating disorders are progressive illnesses. Commonly, we discover that if abstinence is lost and we go back to compulsive overeating, we have even less control than we did previously. Continuing to work the program every day maintains our physical, emotional, and spiritual resources at a high level. Looking good on the outside is wonderful, but it is not enough to ensure continued recovery. Abstinence is an inside condition that gives our self-esteem a tremendous boost.

Frightened when she began purging again, Jane returned to O.A. and her program. "I finally understood what I had heard before, that we have a daily reprieve from our illness, but it is dependent on our spiritual condition. To stay spiritually alive and healthy, we have to keep growing. I got a sponsor and did a Fourth Step. It became clear that I didn't really feel good about my job. I was doing it more to please my father than for any other reason, and I felt resentful and insecure. Once my Higher Power and I got together about what I should be doing, I was able to eat reasonably and stop bingeing and purging. It's nice now to hear someone say I look good, but it's even nicer to feel good, all the way through!"

Abstinence Is Progress

There are days when everything seems out of sync. You oversleep because you forget to set the alarm; your car suddenly develops an ominous squeak; all the parking spaces are filled when you get to work; and so on. If we can reach the end of one of these days without retreating to food, we should consider that marvelous progress.

My friend Peter S. came into O.A. fifteen years ago. For as long as he could remember, he had been overweight. Almost all of his relatives were overweight. The family lifestyle was to have huge meals, which Peter gradually abandoned during his years in the program.

"I made a new circle of friends and stopped spending every holiday with my family. When I did go to see my parents or my brothers and sisters, I'd purposely keep the visits short so I wouldn't get sucked back into the family eating pattern.

"I tried to sell the program to them, but there weren't any takers. It seemed to me they all did their best to sabotage my weight loss. You know—they were always urging me to forget my food plan and celebrate 'just this once.'

"Then last summer, my folks rented a big beach house and invited us all to come for a week—nine adults and six children. It was to be a family reunion. My brother would be back from three years in the Far East, and two of my sisters had birthdays that week.

"I definitely had my doubts about going. I knew there would be problems, and not with just food. Every time I get together with that crowd, I feel like a colossal failure. My brother and brothers-in-law all make much more money than I do. Although most of the family are digging their graves with their forks, I end up feeling that they're successful and I'm not. I get resentful. Everybody is trying to one-up the other, and there's a huge amount of verbal sparring.

"Well, I went anyway. It was a very long week. But I didn't break my abstinence. Before I went, I found out about an O.A. group in a nearby town and got to two meetings during those seven days. That helped tremendously. I could let off steam to people who understood.

"I know now that I can't change my family. I can only work on myself. And I don't have to eat because of what I don't like about what other people say or do."

That Peter was able to maintain his abstinence throughout a difficult situation says volumes for the firm grounding he had in program principles. It's a foundation he had built over fifteen years. For many of the days and weeks and months of those fifteen years, Peter had thought he was standing still.

The payoff came when he faced a highly stressful time and did not relapse. He didn't do as well as he would have liked in maintaining emotional serenity, but he gratefully settled for progress rather than perfection.

What about the times when we're abstinent but can't lose the weight we want to? This happens to many of us, and it's easy to become discouraged.

First, let's remember that O.A. is not a diet club, and the Twelve Steps do not promise quick weight loss. They promise much more—a new way of living. Weight loss may be slow, and we may go through periods when the excess pounds refuse to budge. For me, one of the program's most liberating gifts was allowing me to put away my bathroom scale. I know whether or not I am abstinent without looking at the scale.

While many of us enter this program solely to lose weight, we find before long that this is too narrow a goal. The day will come when the extra pounds are gone, but the need for abstinence remains.

Second, let's remember that body types are different. If you are continually frustrated by not being able to reach your weight goal you may have set that goal too low for your particular body type. If in doubt about your ideal weight range, consult your physician. What seems glamorous on the pages of a fashion magazine may not translate into a realistic or desirable standard for you.

Another possibility, of course, is that your three meals a day are larger than they should be. Abstinence from compulsive eating means moderate meals. If meals become binges, or even mini-binges, that is not abstinence.

Each of us is unique. We need to find what works for us. The program gives us guidelines based on the successful experience of recovering people. We are free to take what we like and leave the rest. Many Twelve Steppers say that when they keep coming back to meetings, and continue asking for help from sponsors and others who have traveled a similar path, they find what they need.

I know a woman who came into the program out of control. (I guess that's the way most of us arrive.) For three months she concentrated on not bingeing, period. Her definition of abstinence then was not bingeing. She was trying to establish a new pattern of sane eating—eating three moderate meals a day and not bingeing. She could worry about losing weight later. After four months, she had neither gained nor lost, but she had not been standing still. She had broken the binge-diet syndrome and for the first time in twenty years could put food in its proper place.

Use It or Lose It

Working the Steps keeps us in motion. We act as we move through them. We accept. We come to believe. We decide, admit, become ready, ask, become willing, seek, pray, try, and practice. There is always more to be done, new insights to add to our understanding, and more courage to take the kinds of risks that will foster spiritual growth.

Steps Ten, Eleven, and Twelve—continuing to take a personal inventory, praying and meditating, and carrying our message to others—all have been called the maintenance part of the program. To maintain our abstinence and healthy spiritual state, we have to keep moving. Since we are always one bite away from a binge, we can't rest on the laurels of yesterday's program.

What are we doing today to keep our program fresh and vital? Most likely, we are continuing to examine our behavior, our attitudes, and our relationships with others. Many of us take a daily inventory during quiet moments before bedtime. If we admit our mistakes the day we become aware of them, there usually is no build up of guilt and resentment to deal with later.

We are seeking to grow spiritually by setting aside time for making contact with our Higher Power. When we do this daily, we are moving in the right direction. Although we may not know exactly where we're headed, we develop trust that we'll be given guidance when we need it. Praying to a Higher Power means we are willing to trust the outcome of the guidance we receive, even if we can't foresee specific events.

The spiritual awakening promised through the Steps is not something that happens once and is over, though some of us may be able to recall a particularly dramatic experience. Our spiritual awakening continues as long as we live. We encourage this to occur by carrying the message to others and practicing the Twelve Step principles in our daily lives. We use the program so that we don't lose it.

We don't stand still. We become "pilgrim[s] who need only [our] marching orders and strength and guidance for this day."[1] The more thoroughly we get into the Steps, the more clearly we realize that life is a journey, sometimes dull, sometimes exciting, sometimes slow, and sometimes rapid. We make the journey one day at a time, "easy does it, but do it."

CHAPTER FIVE

Sliding Down The Tubes

Again—I did it again—sank into that black misery called a binge. How did it happen? Things were going so well! Did I get overconfident? Careless? Why didn't I remember that I never stop at one spoonful of yogurt at four in the afternoon?

Around A.A. meeting rooms they say, "If you can't remember your last drunk, it probably isn't your last." Many of us in O.A. believe that can be applied to binges as well: If you can't remember your last binge, you may not have had it yet. Well, I remember my last binge vividly, so I'm hoping it is indeed my last.

It happened the day after Thanksgiving in November 1985. As I said earlier, I had been divorced at the beginning of the year and had become seriously involved with a very nice man. The relationship's honeymoon stage was wonderful, but then we got down to mundane matters of real life, such as how do we spend money? How do we spend our free time? What happens when one likes to go to bed early and the other prefers to stay up late? Who is going to take out the trash? How much emotional closeness and intimacy is enough, and how much is threatening?

Because the issues were not resolved, the relationship ended in August of 1985. So I was back on my own, feeling sorry for myself, and looking for consolation. And where do you suppose I looked? Well, of course, I looked to my first love, food.

The binges weren't so bad initially. I merely added a little here and there. I was going through a tough time, I rationalized, and a few small additions weren't all that serious.

But my problem started months before the relationship broke up, when I stopped attending meetings regularly. I told myself I didn't really have an eating disorder. Because I had this lovely relationship, I no longer needed to go to meetings.

During September and October my abstinence got sloppier and sloppier. By November I went on major binges at least once a week. In despair, I watched my clothes get tighter and tighter. I became more depressed. Everything was out of control.

What had happened to my program? I found many excuses not to go to meetings: I was too tired, it was raining, my children, or parents, or Prince Charming might call (if he did, I looked and felt too awful to see him). I had already binged when I got home from work so what was the use of attending a meeting?

Since I had lost touch with my O.A. friends, I did not make phone calls. But I did read daily from two meditation books. Though I would wake up in the morning feeling lousy from eating too much the day before and be determined not to binge that day, I would come home from work and immediately go to the refrigerator.

I had terrifying visions of everything I had learned over nine years in the program being washed away. Going back to where I had been before O.A. was a nightmare, but I felt I couldn't stop the slide.

I once heard someone compare breaking abstinence to jumping from a top-floor window of a fifty-story building, with the idea of falling only one or two floors. That was what I had tried. I thought I could make a few additions, with no intention of returning to full-scale bingeing. The problem was, once I started falling, I couldn't stop.

Thanksgiving came. My children were with their father, and I had been invited to a friend's home for dinner. I remember getting through that entire day very well and thinking maybe I was back on track. Wouldn't that be great? Thanksgiving 1985 would mark my new beginning of long-term abstinence!

The next day was also a holiday for me, and I had a long list of things I wanted to do at home. As I worked, I thought about how nice it was to have been at someone else's house for Thanksgiving dinner, since that way there were no seductive leftovers in my kitchen. I was feeling good and was pleased to cross off the projects on my list as I completed them.

At four in the afternoon I decided to have a glass of club soda. The bottle was in the refrigerator, and as I opened the door I saw a quart of plain yogurt. What made me think I could open the container, eat a spoonful of yogurt, be satisfied, close the container, and get back to my projects? Insanity—the sheer insanity of the first compulsive bite. I'd had breakfast, I'd had lunch, I was going to have dinner around 6 P.M., and I wasn't even particularly hungry. I just wanted a spoonful of yogurt.

A voice inside was telling me that I'd had an abstinent day and that if I ate a spoonful of yogurt I would no longer be abstinent. Another voice was saying one little spoonful couldn't really matter. A third voice was saying, *What the heck. I want it and I'll have it and that's that.*

So I ate the spoonful of yogurt, and another, and another, until half of the quart was gone. As I replaced the lid, I told myself I would make up for it by eating less dinner. The yogurt would be my dinner protein, and I would have only vegetables and salad at six o'clock.

Rather than go back to my photograph-sorting project, I decided to read a magazine. My thoughts, however, kept returning to the half-empty container of yogurt in the refrigerator, which drew me in its direction like a magnet. By four-thirty I had finished it and was looking around for something else. Over the course of the next hour, "something else" became four pieces of bread and margarine, an entire box of cereal with milk, six ounces of cheese, about a cup of cold rice, and a third of a jar of peanut butter. I know, because I wrote it all down. I keep that piece of paper in one of my kitchen drawers. I don't ever want to forget that binge.

If there had been more cereal and peanut butter available in my house, I probably would have eaten more. Since I was living alone, I had a policy of not keeping much food around. The only reason I had peanut butter was for my son when he came to visit. (Have you heard that one before?)

Many of my binges before O.A. were considerably worse, back when I was eating ice cream by the half gallon, and I'd go out and buy more food. My former binges were always heavy on sugary foods. After I joined the program and first became abstinent, I binged primarily on healthy foods, but a binge is still a binge: out-of-control eating that makes me feel physically, emotionally, and spiritually sick.

Why had I binged the day after Thanksgiving when I had been abstinent throughout the holiday and thought I was off to a new start? Why did I slide away from the program and back into chaos?

Why?

What is it that causes some of us to slip and slide? Why do some Twelve Steppers become abstinent and remain abstinent, while others are off and on? What prevents some of us from having a comfortable, long-term abstinence?

We can probably find as many answers to these questions as there are people with eating disorders. To oversimplify, we are people who use food to try to relieve stress and solve problems. Since we will always have problems and stress, we are continually vulnerable to misusing food. Of course, we cannot go entirely without eating. Each day we "let the tiger out of the cage," so to speak (the tiger being our appetite, our tendency to overeat), and we must cajole, intimidate, or reason with this tiger so that it does not go berserk and threaten to destroy us.

Someone who breaks abstinence has forgotten that the first compulsive bite will usually become a binge. When we slip, it's because we've become careless with our program and are not using the tools. We can say we forgot we are compulsive eaters, that we somehow lost sight of the First Step, being powerless over food and unable to manage our own lives. We can say we tried again to manage our lives, ignoring our Higher Power and our past history. We can say we are human and make mistakes. We can always find a reason.

To try to determine why abstinence seems more difficult for some than for others may not be all that helpful. We learn this program more by practice and example than by trying to figure it out in our heads. We need to act our way into right thinking. A suggestion we frequently hear is to seek out those individuals who are working a strong program, spend time with them, listen to them, and learn. We're each coming from a unique place and moving at our own pace. We must each start where we are and go from there.

In my case, it took finally coming to the gut-level realization that abstinence must be my number one priority or everything else in my life is at risk. Early on, I accepted that intellectually, but it would slip my mind. Fortunately, many overeaters come into the program and accept the results of other people's experiences without having to reinvent the wheel. For those of you who, like me, have been off and on, all I can say is, "Keep coming back!" Just think where we'd be if we didn't.

Absolutely nothing guarantees I won't slide down the tubes again. If I do, I will probably know why. I believe that my abstinence is dependent on my spiritual condition, and my spiritual condition depends on how closely I stay in touch with my Higher Power and how faithfully I practice the program's Steps.

When abstinent, I wake up with an inner lightness, a sense that all is well. But when I'm not abstinent, I'm depressed. I wake up at three in the morning full of anxiety; no one else can lift that depression. I can't be happy with anyone else unless I am happy with myself, and to be happy with myself, I must be abstinent.

When we focus only on externals—whether they be people, places, or things—we lose sight of our inner goals and strengths.

When we slip and slide, something else has become more important than working the program.

Danger Zones and Slippery Places

Although we may never fully understand a slip, we can try to be on the lookout for potential trouble. Let's examine some of the attitudes, conditions, and circumstances that may be dangerous. Forewarned is forearmed!

An excellent warning signal is the acronym we have adapted from the A.A. program—HALT. Never get too Hungry, too Angry, too Lonely, or too Tired. Any one of these conditions can trigger a binge.

Skipping meals is not a good idea. Our bodies will protest and want to overcompensate with too much food the next time it's available. As for anger, we should try to identify it when we feel it, find a constructive way to express it, and then let go of it.

We will each feel lonely occasionally, but too much loneliness can be harmful. We need to seek the companionship of people we enjoy, instead of trying to ease our loneliness by overeating.

If I wrote a book titled, *Binges I Have Known*, one chapter would be devoted to the close relation between binges and fatigue. Getting tired is an automatic cue prompting me to think I need food. Formerly, I often used food, especially sugar, as a quick pick-up. It worked initially, but then more and more was required to do the picking up, until the reverse reaction occurred: more fatigue than I had felt before I started to eat. Getting too tired lowered my resolve to maintain abstinence and made manageable tasks seem overwhelming. The ultimate result of a binge was that I got the rest I needed, since I was too zonked to do anything but sleep. The trick is to remember, before taking that first compulsive bite, that rest is the cure for fatigue, not food.

Ideally, practicing HALT may keep us from getting too tired in the first place. Many times we get greedy for experiences and accomplishments, wanting to have it all and do it all. That's impossible, and it puts our abstinence in jeopardy. When abstinence is our number one priority, then unnecessary activity that wears us out has to go.

The flip side of too much activity is boredom, another pitfall for compulsive overeaters. How many times have you decided to eat something because you couldn't think of anything else to do?

When a flat, blah feeling looms up before us, let's beware that we don't mistakenly translate it into hunger. Let's also work on developing the genuine friendships, interests, vocational commitments, hobbies, and relationships that keep our lives full and vital.

My friend, Anne, says certain people she knows are hazardous to her abstinence, so she avoids them whenever possible. If contact is necessary, she makes sure it will be for only a short time, and she may arrange to talk afterward with a sympathetic friend. That way she can express her reactions and feelings and get feedback and help, rather than risk a binge.

Most of us who develop eating disorders do so because we're out of touch with how we really feel. When we don't want to experience negative emotions such as sadness, hurt, fear, and anger, we try to stifle them with food. Not eating—the self-starvation of anorexia—is also a way of stifling emotions.

When we stop communicating out loud to the people who can give us support, bright yellow caution lights should begin to flash in front of our eyes. Is it pride that makes us think we should be able to solve our problems by ourselves? Going over and over the same issues in our heads is confusing, emotionally distressing, and sets us up for a slip.

Feeling sorry for ourselves—now, there's a tempting reason to break abstinence! As a college student, I remember sitting at home on Saturday night without a date, eating the sweet rolls my roommate and I had bought for Sunday breakfast and then going out to buy more. I didn't know what abstinence was then. Even when I did know, I remember breaking it because I felt sorry for myself. For example, once I stayed at home while the rest of the family went on a ski trip. I had chosen not to go on the trip. Instead of eating, why didn't I find something fun to do?

Playing the role of the martyr—do you have a hard time saying no, even when the other person's request is clearly inconvenient or unreasonable? "It's not my turn to clean up the apartment, but you have another commitment and we're having a party tonight, so I'll do it (and I'll eat)." Do you let yourself be a doormat and then get even by sabotaging your program?

Or we might be cocky and overconfident. "I've got it down pat now. This is a snap. Abstinence is easy." Need we say more? Ours is a simple program, but easy? No.

Slippery places. Among those that come to my mind are bakeries, certain sections of the grocery store, ice cream parlors, all-you-can-eat restaurants, and leftovers. A very slippery situation for me is a family meal where there is conflict, whether it's out in the open or hidden. Another is coming home after a disappointing day or evening. Where are your slippery places?

A slippery substance for me is alcohol. Although my drug of choice has always been excess food, at one point I also drank too much. Since I know that alcohol can easily trigger a binge, I put alcoholic beverages in the category of binge foods and avoid them.

We've talked about dangerous attitudes, situations, places, and actions—things we do that get us into trouble. What about the things we don't do that may send us sliding down the tubes? What heads my list is not remembering I have an eating disorder. From that, disaster follows. I don't go to meetings, I don't make food plans, I don't use the tools of the program, I don't depend on my Higher Power—in short, I don't work my program. And then I'm in a highly dangerous, extremely slippery, life-threatening place.

Where Is Bottom?

When we start sliding, where do we stop? How far down must we go before the only direction in which we can move is up? How far down was your bottom? Have you hit it yet?

People die of eating disorders, some quickly and some slowly. "I was bingeing and purging ten times a day," says Alice. "I hated myself. One afternoon I was trying to pack my things to go to Florida where I thought maybe I could start all over. I looked at myself in the mirror, and I knew I was going to die if I didn't get help."

Steve doesn't know how much he weighed, but he knows it was more than 400 pounds. "I couldn't climb a flight of stairs without getting completely out of breath and shaky. My doctor told me my blood pressure was dangerously high and that I was high risk for a heart attack. I didn't want to live."

"I was only ten pounds overweight," says Laura, "but I had lost and regained those same ten pounds hundreds of times. All I could think about was food. I thought about it every waking moment. I was obsessed. Food controlled my life."

Where is bottom? I think it's the place where we surrender, wave a white flag, accept that we can't manage our illness or our lives by ourselves, and become willing to go to any length to recover.

The number of pounds you weigh does not determine where bottom will be found, because compulsive behavior with food, eating, weight, and diets can occur at any number on the scale. The obsession can control someone who is underweight, normal weight, or overweight.

The only requirement for membership in a Twelve-Step program for overeaters is the desire to stop eating compulsively. If you weigh 300 pounds, you may find it hard to believe that Gail who weighs 110 has a problem with food. To you, she looks wonderful. What you may not know is that Gail takes an average of 75 laxatives a week so she won't gain weight from her binges.

Keep Coming Back

Here's what other recovering overeaters said:

"Bottom was when my six-year-old son asked me not to come to see the school program he was in, because he didn't want his friends to know how fat I was."

"Bottom was when I knew if I didn't get help, I would kill myself."

"Bottom was when I got sick and tired of being sick and tired."

"For me, bottom was when I realized where I was headed and decided I didn't want to go there."

"Bottom was when I had tried everything else, and all that was left to try was a Higher Power."

CHAPTER SIX

After The Fall

Wherever the bottom is for you, you hit it with a thud. And then what do you do?

The bottom you hit may be the one that introduces you to the Twelve Step program for overeaters. You may "catch" the program, become abstinent, and never slide down those tubes again. That happens for some people; when it does we should rejoice. Nevertheless, O.A. invites you to keep coming back since continuing to work the program is our best insurance against relapse.

Unfortunately, for most of us, relapses do occur. Eating disorders are chronic illnesses, and we should not consider ourselves failures when we slip and slide. We are assured that in this program, there are no failures, only slow successes. Some of us require more time than others. As long as we're honestly working the program to the best of our ability, we keep the door open for progress. "Life only demands from you the strength you possess. Only one feat is possible—not to have run away."[1]

When we quit, give up, run away, and stay away from the shared experience—the strength and hope we gain from others who struggle with a similar problem—we shut the door on potential recovery. Above all, this we do not want to do.

What do we do after the fall? We pick ourselves up, dust ourselves off, make a food plan, call a sponsor, get to a meeting, and start again. How many times do we do this? As many times as it takes. Ask yourself, *what is the alternative?*

Most of us come to O.A. as a last resort. I certainly did. Before I was willing to consider a one-day-at-a-time commitment to abstinence and the Twelve Steps, I tried every other way I could find. I tried the diets, the self-help books, exercise clubs, diet clubs, and spas. I promised myself new clothes if I could lose another ten pounds. I took courses on how to meditate, yoga, and psychiatry—you name it, I tried it. When I slipped and fell, there was nowhere left for me to go except back to abstinence and the Twelve Steps. I knew the other ways didn't work for me, and I knew the program did work for me when I worked it. I remembered how wonderful I had felt when I was abstinent, and I wanted to feel that way again.

As I see it, after the fall we have two options: (1) We can give up, quit, and return to the misery of slow (or not so slow) self-destruction; or (2) we can try again.

Picking Yourself Up

There's one good thing about my eating disorder. It keeps me humble and aware of my need for a Higher Power. If I start thinking I can control my food problem and my life on my own, that is precisely when I'm headed for trouble. First the pride; then the fall. And after the fall, I go back to where I should have stayed in the first place, back to asking God to take over.

Specifically, we go back to Steps One through Three. We have proven again (and we hope this time the proof will be conclusive) that we are powerless over food and are unable to manage our lives without a Power greater than ourselves. We have a program that we know will work if we're willing to make a new commitment to abstinence and the Twelve Steps—a new commitment to use the tools at our disposal.

Willing to Go to Any Lengths

Relapse can be a minor slip, a major slide, or any point in-between. When we take minor slips seriously rather than ignoring them, we have a better chance of preventing them from becoming major disasters. How easy it is to say, Well, I ate more than I should have today, but it was a tough day.

Since I've already broken my abstinence, I might as well have some _____(you fill in the blank). A few of those tough day excuses and we're headed for big trouble. If we've had a major slide, we must guard against further punishing ourselves. At any point on the relapse scale, we may turn around, converting an abstinent moment into an abstinent hour, an abstinent day, week, month, year, and the rest of a lifetime.

"I'm willing to go to any lengths to recover." This is the winner's mind-set. Is it yours? What does it mean in terms of concrete actions to rebuild your program?

After the despair of my last binge put me back in touch with my Higher Power, the first thing I did was write a food plan for the next day. I hadn't written a food plan for more than a year because I thought I was beyond the need for that kind of discipline. Obviously, I wasn't.

Planning my meals in my head is not as concrete nor as helpful as writing the items on paper. Writing a food plan forces me to make decisions I might otherwise leave hanging in limbo. It also makes it harder to rationalize making additions based on impulse and hunger when mealtime arrives.

Writing a food plan for the next day was easy after that last binge because I wasn't hungry. It was a simple matter to list moderate amounts of healthy foods. The way I was feeling then, those foods looked like more than enough. But I knew that by six the following evening, my dinner plan would seem sparse. How was I going to stay within the reasonable limits I had set, since I had not done so for a long time? Did that mean I should get a food sponsor again? Call someone? When was the last time I had phoned an O.A. member?

The further from abstinence I got, the harder it was for me to pick up the phone and ask for help. Fortunately, I still had my list of numbers, and something told me they weren't doing a whole lot of good tucked away in my desk drawer. Since I seriously doubted I would follow my food plan for the next day on my own, and I was tired of hurting, I picked up the telephone. Making that call was very much like making my first O.A. phone call, but there was one very important difference: I knew the support I needed would be there if I asked for it. And it was.

For me, "willing to go to any lengths" in 1985 meant getting a food sponsor, calling in my plan every day, making at least one other O.A. phone call each day, going to three meetings a week, and doing a Fourth Step inventory. It worked.

For Linda C., "willing to go to any lengths" included going back to beginner's meetings. Although she had been in the program more than a year, she had lost her abstinence. Now she decided to operate as though she was hearing everything for the first time.

Jack N. decided to follow an A.A. recommendation and go to 90 meetings in 90 days. He lived in a large metropolitan area where many O.A. meetings were available. "It took some fancy planning," Jack said, grinning, "but getting my abstinence back was more than worth it. People asked me how I managed to have time for my social life. I told them with all of those meetings I didn't need any more social life."

For Carolyn T., the problem was dinner. She lived alone. Breakfast was okay. "I never binged in the morning," she explains. "I had lunch in the school cafeteria, and that was okay, too, since I never binged in public. It was when I got home in the late afternoon that the battle began. I could usually hold off until dinnertime, but once I started eating I couldn't stop." For a month, Carolyn determined that each evening she would buy only what she needed for that day's dinner and the next morning's breakfast. "It worked," she reported. "It was a nuisance, but it worked. After a month I had broken the dinner-binge-binge-binge habit, and I gradually began to keep extra food in the house again."

"Willing to go to any lengths" includes working Steps we might prefer to ignore. That might mean concrete action to carry out Step Nine, making direct amends wherever possible to the people we have harmed. For a compulsive overeater, it's

tough to harbor guilt and resentment while maintaining abstinence. We receive the strength needed to live with confidence
one day at a time by shedding the burden of negative thoughts
and feelings that oppress our spirit.

"I realized I was still overeating due to a disappointing relationship with my sister," Pat F. told me. "If I wanted a change,
I was the one who was going to have to do something. I wrote
a letter, accepting responsibility for my share of the conflict. I
told my sister I was sorry. I won't say our relationship was
miraculously mended, but it did improve. Most important, I
felt relieved of a lot of garbage—anger and hurt and guilt—
from way back. I didn't have to eat over it anymore."

When we were into food, to what lengths did we go to get
our fix? While attending college, I stole food from the dor-
mitory kitchen and from other people's rooms. To what lengths
did we go to keep our binges a secret? How did we rearrange
our lives to accommodate our habit? To what lengths will we
go to get well?

Learning

I think we learn more from our mistakes than from our
successes. Since we've agreed there are no failures in this program, let's talk about mistakes instead.

It would be nice if we could work the program perfectly the
first time, but we're not perfect. Many people with eating disorders discover that pefectionism is part of the illness. *The Best
Little Girl in the World*, a book that was made into a television
play, tells the story of a teenage girl who was both anorexic
and bulimic. How many of us tried to be "the best little girl in
the world"? How many of us, male or female, are still trying
to do things perfectly?

Women in our society are particularly vulnerable to developing eating disorders. We might think we should be able to
do it all and have it all—a happy family, a successful career, a
perfect body, and cultural and leisure-time pursuits. Yet, the
role models are unclear. Some of us may think we're supposed

to do more than our mothers did and do it better. Dieting is a national obsession and, before we found O.A., we possibly thought we should do that perfectly too.

O.A. is not another diet-and-calories club. Although abstinence is different, we may go at it with our customary perfectionistic mind-set. Then, if we slip, we're convinced we've failed, because we haven't done it perfectly. We berate ourselves for having failed to be 100 percent abstinent. Then we feel so depressed that the only solution seems to be more food.

This can be an often repeated scenario if we're caught in the trap of perfectionism with its impossible demands. The wonderful freedom of the Twelve Step program is that we come to know a Higher Power who does not expect us to be perfect. That means we can stop expecting it of ourselves.

Tearing ourselves down should definitely not be part of the recovery process. Nor should impatience. Our problems with food didn't suddenly emerge yesterday, and they probably won't vanish tomorrow. We should be as patient with ourselves as we would be with a baby who is learning to walk. After all, we're learning a new way of life, and we need all the help and support we can get. We need to be able to explore the adventure of abstinence, and if we don't make it the first time, to try again. And again. And again.

Whether minor or major, a slip is a learning experience. At the very least, we learn what does not work. Going back to my experience from "Binges I Have Known," I can give you some examples of what does not work for me.

1. *Going to the grocery store before mealtime, when I am hungry.* More than once, this has been my downfall. Either I have bought items not in my food plan, or I have come home with large quantities, or I binged before I could get the food put away. I do best if I go to the store early in the day when I have lots of energy and I can resist harmful impulses. I understand that now, after being convinced by several very unhappy binges.

2. *Cleaning up after a party when I'm tired and alone.* A kitchen is not a good place for me to be if I am tired and alone. I can

spend more time eating than cleaning up. I have eaten party leftovers and gone on to find something more. I've found it's better to let the clean-up job wait until morning when I have a greater chance of doing it without sabotaging my program.

3. *Consuming alcohol.* I've spent many years learning that alcohol does strange things to my appetite. I can have a glass of wine with dinner, maintain my abstinence for that evening, and be out of control the next afternoon. I'm not sure why this occurs, but it has happened enough times for me to know that alcohol is hazardous to my abstinence.

The list could go on and on, but so much for examples of what not to do. A second learning area is related to what I have found out about myself—in particular, why I spent so much time using food to try to solve problems food can't solve. An example of this kind of learning comes from another prospective book title, *My Good Mother Is Not in the Refrigerator.*

Unfortunately, mothers are the most readily available hooks on which to hang the origin of an eating disorder, since they have traditionally been responsible for the care and feeding of infants and children. I was a child and I am a mother, and I am well aware of how easy it is to blame a mother for too much or too little attention, understanding, affection, discipline, and other qualities that mothers are supposed to give in precise amounts.

My mother would be the first to admit that she, being human and fallible, made mistakes with me, and I will as readily accept responsibility for errors and inadequacies in the mothering I have done.

One thing I've learned from my slips is that, when bingeing, I was trying to find my warm, caring, supporting, understanding mother in the refrigerator. A strange place to look? Not really. As a child, I associated pleasing Mother with eating all of my supper and drinking all of my milk. I associated warmth and caring and affection with being fed. If something hurt, physically or emotionally, food would often make it feel better. My mother expressed love by making cookies, cakes, rolls, pies, and souffles. Making a batch of fudge or getting in the car and going for ice cream cones were favorite family activities.

In a child's eyes, mind, and heart, Mother is good when she is cheerful, warm, loving, happy. She is not good when she is tired, preoccupied, angry, upset. Consequently, for me, food was the magic substance that evoked my good mother; whenever I was in need of soothing or consolation or support, I searched the refrigerator.

I started doing this when I was eleven. To this day, almost 40 years later, I still find myself moving toward the kitchen when I feel a need for comfort, support, reassurance, courage, or even just for fun! Sometimes I get as far as opening the refrigerator door and looking inside before I remember my good mother is not there anymore.

Once, soothing myself with food served a purpose—it was the best way I could find to deal with problems and emotional pain. Now I've learned that I have better ways of coping with my problems, with anxiety, anger, sadness, frustration, and hurt. I know now I can get the comfort and support I need from my Higher Power and from other people, and that, when necessary, I can even be my own good mother.

I have recognized my tendency to want to escape into eating when the going gets rough. In this sense, my eating disorder has been a cop-out from facing whatever is uncomfortable. Conflict, challenge, intimacy, failure, mortality, hard work— all can be uncomfortable, and something inside of me used to imagine that if I ate enough these problems and challenges would go away. But they did not disappear. After a binge, I would be even less able to deal with them. All I had done was anesthetize myself temporarily, but the issues remained.

After my fall down the tubes in November of 1985, I realized I had not come to terms emotionally with being divorced and single. I was looking for a man to care for me, and instead of accepting the challenge of learning who I was on my own, I was escaping into food. When I was married, I ate to avoid conflict and the problems of intimacy. When I became single, I ate to avoid the anxiety of being alone.

Through recovering from a relapse, we gain new insight into old patterns of thought and behavior, and we learn how we can change. We do not have to repeat the same mistakes. We have a support network of others who have traveled the same path, we have Steps to guide us, and we have strength from a Power greater than ourselves. If we slip, all is not lost. We can come back and try again. We can keep coming back as many times as are necessary.

Perhaps the most important learning of all is that we need each other for recovery. When we think we can get along without meetings and phone calls and sharing, when we think we can do it alone, we are treading on dangerous territory. Eating disorders encourage withdrawal and isolation; recovery brings us together. We don't graduate from the Twelve Step program. We keep coming back.

CHAPTER SEVEN

Where's Home Base?

Ours is a spiritual program. This is what makes it different from a diet-and-calories club. This is how we get the strength to abstain from compulsive eating or dieting, one day at a time. We build our spiritual strength little by little, day by day. Because we have a spiritual program, we handle difficult situations without resorting to food abuse. Before O.A. we may have felt and acted as though we were lost out in left field, but now we have an idea about where home base might be.

We know there is an alternative to bingeing (or starving), a better way to deal with problems. Even, and especially, if we relapse, we remember how good we felt when we were abstaining. We want to get back to abstinence. Our binges nudge us back slowly or propel us back rapidly to the O.A. program.

After the fall, we want to rebuild on a solid foundation so we won't continue to slide. I've never really lost what I had previously built up; I merely moved away from it. But I needed to reinforce and strengthen my program so that I would stay with it, in spite of pressures and distractions.

We all need a safe place to go when we get tired and discouraged or jangled by too many external things bombarding our senses. We need a retreat for the times when anxiety turns our thoughts toward extra food. We need a solid home base, a place where we can get in touch with our inner voice and our Higher Power.

For many years, the physical location of home base for me has been a comfortable, blue upholstered chair. When I was married, the chair was placed in front of a window in the corner of a small study. After my former husband and I separated, I moved, and the blue chair is now in front of another window, in another small study.

I've spent some of my best moments in that chair. When I began to work seriously on Step Eleven, prayer and meditation, the blue chair became my spot for a few minutes in the morning and the evening. It continues to be the place where I go when I need to mentally and emotionally sort things out, when I have wandered far from my center and have lost the sound of my inner voice. Now, even when things are going well and I'm feeling happy, it's a good place to be for a few minutes.

But home base is not limited to any specific geographical location. Home base can be instantly shifted to a motel room if I'm traveling, my car, a park bench, the desk chair in my office, a church pew, my kitchen sink, or a grassy spot under a tree.

Home base is wherever I am in contact with the God of my understanding. It is a state of mind, a spiritual condition. Home base is where I stop carrying the world on my shoulders, regretting the past, worrying about the future, and where I say, "Okay, God—I give up. Your will, not mine."

David's Story

David L. has been in the program for three years. He says he's been a compulsive overeater most of his life:

"My father is an alcoholic. When I was about twelve, I promised myself I would never drink, but I used food exactly the way my father uses alcohol.

"The first time I went to an O.A. meeting, I knew I was in the right place. I got a sponsor and started working the Steps. Abstinence, though, just didn't come. I'd have a few good days, and then something would set me off and I'd be right back into the food.

"I was spending loads of time and energy trying to 'fix' my parents, and I wasn't getting that much better myself. I was still bingeing at least once a week. Food was my prop. It always had been. Whenever I got tense or mad or depressed, I wanted to eat.

"When I was growing up, things were usually in an uproar at our house. My father would get drunk and yell at my mother, and she yelled back. They fought almost constantly.

"When we ate meals together, my mother was usually nagging my father. I kept very quiet and tried to just think about eating. Sometimes, on the rare occasions when my father wasn't drinking, mealtimes would be good—almost happy. In fact, the best memories I have of the three of us together are all associated with food. My mother was a great cook and a compulsive eater.

"Mother made special treats for me—that was how she showed her love. I tried to defend her against my father's criticism and anger, but I only got caught in the middle. I would wake up at night and hear them fighting. Sometimes I'd slip down to the kitchen and get cookies out of a big, tin box my mom kept filled. I can't remember a time when I wasn't overweight.

"About six months ago, something really clicked for me. I had come home after visiting my mom and dad and, as usual, I was in a bad mood, and, as usual, I hit the food. I was standing in the kitchen at ten in the evening with a bowl of cold macaroni and cheese, and suddenly it dawned on me that as long as I kept bingeing I would never be able to grow up emotionally and move away from the pain of my childhood, over which I had absolutely no control.

"I realized I was still powerless over what my mother and my father did and their relationship with each other. As long as I ate compulsively, I was still trying to 'fix' it, and I would never be able to do that.

"That was a revelation. At the same time, I also understood that I had a source of spiritual strength that I did not have as a child. My Higher Power does not expect me to solve my parents' problems. I can't force them into a Twelve Step program, but I can keep building my spiritual strength so I don't get sucked back into the insanity of addiction."

David says he has had clean abstinence since that evening six months ago.

"Food is no longer a problem. It never was the problem. Living was the problem. Now, when I think about eating something I don't need, something that's not part of my food plan, I ask myself if I want to go back to the inner chaos and confusion I felt when growing up. The answer is no, so I don't overeat. I'm under a lot of stress now, for various reasons, and the only way I am strong enough to handle it is by maintaining abstinence and turning to my Higher Power to get me through a tough situation."

For David, as for so many of us, food was a home base when he was growing up. Food, of course, was not enough. Through working the program he was able to build a stronger base, a spiritual base. David's turning point came when he could apply Step One to his painful, tangled relationship with his parents.

"Now I'm working on applying the rest of the Steps to that relationship. Since I'm not bingeing, I've gained some distance and detachment. One day at a time, I'm leaving the results to God."

Susan's Story

In high school Susan was anorexic and bulimic. She was in therapy for years, which helped, and when she went to college she joined O.A. She says:

"For eighteen months, I did well with the program, and then my boyfriend dumped me. We had gone together for almost four years—all through college—and when he told me he was moving to California and wanted to be on his own, I was devastated. I lost seventeen pounds the month after graduation. I stopped eating and went down to 90 pounds. I was sure my life was over. I wanted to die.

"I had been depending on Kevin to take care of me. My major was art history. I had planned that I was going to paint and Kevin was going to be a successful businessman who would support me. When Kevin said he wanted out, I was terrified. What was I going to do?

"Every night when I went to bed I told myself that tomorrow I'd start thinking about looking for a job (I was living with my parents) but the next day I'd be too tired and too depressed to do anything. I fantasized about how Kevin would see he'd made a mistake and come back from California, we'd get married, and everything would be okay. But he never called or answered my letters.

"One night in August I called him. I was so upset—really hysterical. I said I was going to kill myself. He hung up. I called him back, and a girl answered the phone and said Kevin had gone out.

"I was devastated. I was going to swallow every pill in the house and was just opening the door of the upstairs medicine cabinet when the phone rang.

"It was Yvonne, the woman who had been my sponsor in O.A. until she went to Spain on a six month study program. She had been back a couple of weeks, hadn't seen me at the meeting, and was calling to see how I was doing. Talk about a Higher Power! Mine was certainly looking out for me then.

"When I tried to talk to Yvonne, all I could do was cry. She made me promise to stay at my house until she got there. Yvonne came, and after a while I calmed down enough to tell her what had happened. She stayed with me that night. The next day we talked and talked, and she finally convinced me to call the therapist I had seen when I was in high school and make an appointment. Then she got me to go to an O.A. meeting with her.

"I don't remember much about the next few weeks, except that I decided Kevin was not worth dying for. I felt as if God must want me to live for some reason, and my job was to learn why.

"After that, I began to see more clearly how insane my behavior was, and gradually my belief in a Higher Power became stronger. Before, I didn't depend on God and I didn't think I could depend on myself, so I depended on the fantasy I had of Kevin, who was going to take care of me. Once I was able to see what an illusion that was, I got back on a reasonable food plan and began getting back to a normal weight.

"I still freaked out sometimes when I saw the numbers on the scale go up. Several times I was tempted to go back to purging when I saw how much weight I was gaining—in high school I had made myself throw up almost every day. Sometimes I got very scared that I would keep gaining and gaining and would look gross. I still had this crazy idea that if I was thin enough, I'd get Kevin back.

"I talked about all this, especially with my therapist and my O.A. friends. I know now that as long as I talk with others I'm going to be okay. It's when I don't talk to anyone that I'm really in trouble.

"I do believe my Higher Power is taking care of me, which has made a big difference in my life. Otherwise, I wouldn't have had the courage to finally go out and get a job and begin to make decisions on my own. Before, I asked Kevin about every little move I made. I leaned on Kevin because I thought I couldn't make it without him. Now I've got my own support system. I have at least five good friends I can call whenever I need to talk."

Like David, Susan was learning that underneath her eating disorder were important, unresolved issues that she had to face and deal with as part of her recovery. Merely focusing on what she did or did not eat was not enough. Coming to believe in a Power greater than herself was the foundation on which she could build healthy independence and strength. Once she felt a deep confidence that a Higher Power was taking care of her, she had her own internal home base.

Kate's Story

If Kate hadn't found O.A. when she did, she says she's sure Mike and she would be divorced by now. They still may split, but they're in much better shape now than they were a year ago. A year ago Kate took Step One, admitting she was powerless over food. She says:

"I spent more time eating than doing anything else. I was sure it was all Mike's fault. I held him personally responsible for everything that went wrong in my life, everything I didn't like, including the fact that I weighed 223 pounds. It seemed natural to me to blame Mike—my mother always blamed my father for just about everything, except maybe the weather.

"I did fine with the first three Steps, but I had a tough time with Step Four! Me, taking an inventory? I thought I had all the answers. There wasn't anything wrong with me except my lousy husband and crazy kids. It took several meetings before I would even consider the idea that the only person I could change was myself.

"I kept nagging, trying to change everyone else, until one of my friends in O.A. said she didn't become abstinent until she did a Fourth Step. I figured I might as well give it a try. That was when I began to get a glimmer of how I could possibly do some housecleaning on myself and my character defects. I didn't really think it would work, but by the time I took a personal inventory and shared it with someone, I was already making some changes. Like occasionally giving my husband and kids credit for the things they did right.

"I saw that I had always resented Mike because his family was better off than mine—he'd had a lot of advantages I didn't. Then, too, I was very jealous. I figured other women were bound to be more attractive to him than 223 pounds of me. Even if he didn't say anything, I thought he was putting me down in his head. I guess I felt insecure from the very beginning of the marriage. The more insecure I felt, the more I ate. The more I ate, the worse I looked, and the worse I looked the worse I felt, and the worse I felt the more I ate and the more I nagged.

"I kept going with the Steps. By the time I got to Eight, I was losing weight and following a food plan. Now I'm up to

Nine. I've made my amends list. Mike's on it—my kids too. I'm not expecting any miracles, but I can see some changes.

"Whether we stay married or not, this program has given me a sense of security I never had before. I figure wherever I am is where God wants me to be today, and if I stay in contact with my Higher Power, I'll know where I'm supposed to be tomorrow."

Finding the Center

Where is home base for you? A good way to find out is by practicing the Steps, especially Step Eleven, making conscious contact with our Higher Power. We can spend much time and energy running around the outside of our lives looking for fairy godmothers and magic solutions, but this is a frustrating trip. The fairy godmothers and the magic solutions soon vanish. Our spiritual journey—the journey toward the center—is the one I think brings lasting support and satisfaction.

It's so easy to get lost chasing rainbows. For such a long time, I thought being thin was all I needed to be happy forever. When being thin didn't do it, I thought perhaps achievement, money, or the right relationship would be the answer. Or a combination of all three.

To be sure, there's nothing wrong with achievement, money, the right relationship, or maintaining ideal weight. But they're not enough. They're subject to change, and they don't get us through a sleepless night when a family member has been in a serious accident. They also don't guarantee inner confidence or a healthy self-image.

We might like to think we can get along without a Higher Power. Our own self-will and the culture in which we live often encourage self-sufficiency. But by the time we arrive at a Twelve Step program, most of us have exhausted the possibility of going it alone, without reference to the spiritual dimension in our lives.

Most of us come to the Twelve Step program because we're hurting. Our will and our way just isn't doing the job anymore.

We feel lost and alone and unable to manage. The good news is that when we feel this way, we're open to God's power. When we know we've exhausted our own strength, we become willing to trust a Higher Power because there isn't any other alternative.

Only when we let go of weak props and false securities and become humble enough to trust the God of our understanding do we arrive at home base and begin to find our spiritual center. We have to keep finding it every day, many times a day, and it's an exciting time of exploration and discovery.

You say you've tried Step Eleven, prayer and meditation, and it doesn't work. How often have you tried it? Every day for the past three months? No? Then why don't you make a contract with yourself (and your Higher Power) that you will spend fifteen minutes a day for the next three months "centering" yourself?

Have a definite idea of when and where you will spend these fifteen minutes. The time and location may be subject to change when necessary, but it's useful to establish a regular pattern, especially at the beginning. Reading from a meditation book is a helpful way to start. Then you'll want to spend time reflecting, being quiet, and listening for that inner voice. You may get hooked on your quiet time and find yourself going beyond fifteen minutes. And that's okay. The center is where we come to know ourselves very intimately. I think the closer we get to the center, the more sure we are of being guided and supported by a Higher Power. And I think that the closer we get to our center, the more easily and comfortably we relate to other people.

Each day recovery teaches me that home base is not my scale or my refrigerator or wearing a size eight. Home base is inside of me. It's where I go to make contact with the God of my understanding, to try to discover His will for my life, and to receive the power to carry that out.

CHAPTER EIGHT

Accept No Substitutes

Ideally, through our program we learn how to get to home base through abstinence and the Twelve Steps. Ideally, the program takes hold of us, and if we suffer relapses, they are short ones. Ideally, it does not take us long to become convinced that no amount of food will fill up the empty place inside ourselves that craves spiritual nourishment.

This is what we'd like to see happen, but we often find reality doesn't conform to our ideals. Instead, many of us go through periods when we get hooked into substituting other compulsions for compulsive eating or dieting. This is called transferring obsessions. We may maintain abstinence from compulsive eating but get caught up in compulsive shopping and overspending. We may stop bingeing on food but binge on alcohol or sex or harmful relationships. We may get trapped on a treadmill of compulsive work. Or we may get hooked on drugs—caffeine, nicotine, marijuana, cocaine.

Transferring obsessions means that we are still trying to use substances or "things" or compulsive activity of one kind or another to fill our emptiness and nurture our spirit. We are misled because these substitutes do seem to work temporarily. Frequently, though, the sad end result is another addictive habit that saps our energy and depresses our spirits.

How do we get into these misguided transfer operations, and how do we get out once we're in? More importantly, how can we avoid transferring obsessions in the first place?

Looking for a Magic Substance

I've had considerable experience with alternatives and additions to the food obsession. Although food was always my first love in times of stress, perplexity, boredom, or celebration, there have been numerous other outlets for my compulsive tendencies. Let's talk about substances first. Then we can move on to areas that include "things," work, and relationships.

At one point I was drinking about twenty cups of coffee a day; for at least fifteen years I smoked two packs of cigarettes a day; for sixteen years I consumed an unhealthy amount of alcohol; for twenty years I took tranquilizers regularly; and I tried amphetamines intermittently. I used the caffeine, nicotine, and amphetamines in a vain attempt to boost my energy, control my appetite, look sophisticated, keep my weight down, and prevent bingeing. I took the tranquilizers to relieve symptoms of anxiety, which were made more severe, if not produced, by the other drugs I was loading into my system. I drank alcohol to do all of the above and, especially, to get myself through social situations where I felt uncomfortable.

I was in control, all right! I used coffee and cigarettes and amphetamines to get me revved up and then alcohol and tranquilizers to calm me down. The amphetamines were the first to go. They were exhausting. I was so wound up I would find myself cleaning closets at two A.M.

Getting off the pills wasn't easy, but since I didn't take them for more than a couple of months at a stretch, the only withdrawal effects that I can remember were exhaustion and a ravenous appetite. I took lots of naps and ate lots of food.

Cigarettes went next, several years later. I had stopped smoking twice before the final time, once for eight months when I was pregnant. Each time I stopped I gained so much weight and felt so miserable and depressed that I went back to smoking. Each time I decided to give up cigarettes I promised myself this time it would be different, that I would only smoke a few cigarettes a day in a civilized fashion. Both times it wasn't long before I was back to two packs a day. But when my seven-year-old son started experimenting with my cigarettes, I finally had enough motivation to stop for good. I took deep breaths, chewed gum continually, and gained fifteen pounds.

Several years later I finally parted company with caffeine. I had switched from coffee to tea, but soon I was drinking about twenty cups of tea a day, so I hadn't reduced my caffeine intake. Finally, I went cold turkey and cut out all forms of caffeine and went around like a zombie for at least a month, again taking lots of naps.

So with amphetamines, nicotine, and caffeine out of the way, that left tranquilizers, alcohol, and, of course, food in my arsenal of mood-altering substances. When I started sleeping by myself instead of with my husband, I stopped taking tranquilizers. That says something about me and about the marriage.

I denied drinking too much, and it wasn't until I found O.A. and took Step One (admitting that I was powerless over food) that I realized I was also powerless over alcohol. Drinking alcohol and bingeing had increasingly gone hand in hand. Drinking began as a substitute for bingeing but became, instead of a substitute, a trigger.

Just as drinking and using other drugs often go together, so do drinking and bingeing. We hear about this in the Twelve Step meeting rooms. We hear it from recovering alcoholics who have become compulsive overeaters and bulimics. We hear it from bulimics who use cocaine to lose weight and keep from bingeing. Eating disorders are very similar to chemical dependency. Some of us switch back and forth, and some of us use two or more substances concurrently. The more we take in, the emptier we feel.

Somewhere, we imagine, there must be a magic elixir. We take a few swallows, or a few bites, or a few doses and think, *Wow! I've found it at last! Now I can make myself live happily ever after.* Then the rosy glow we felt at first begins to fade, and we need more and more of the magic substance to produce the glow. Then we get to a point of diminishing returns where more and more makes us feel worse and worse. Why can't we recapture the magic? Is there another place to look?

Reaching for the Brass Ring

When substances don't work, some of us switch to one or more forms of compulsive activity to fill the inner emptiness. We may go on buying sprees, collecting things to satisfy the craving for more. Or we may become compulsive about our work, putting in many hours of overtime at the office each week, or creating tension at home as we obsessively clean, polish, remodel, and redecorate. We can become compulsive about exercise or social activity to the point of exhaustion.

What are we trying to prove? Why are we constantly reaching for more? Why is our self-image so poor that we knock ourselves out trying to prove our worth? Do we really think we can validate ourselves with a closetful of new clothes? A *House Beautiful* interior? Another promotion? Winning a marathon?

I know a woman who joined O.A., lost about 50 pounds, took up jogging, increased her running time each week until she was up to sixteen miles a day, and rearranged her entire life to accommodate that schedule. She was afraid to miss a single day of running sixteen miles. If she stopped, she was sure she would go back to bingeing.

When we're children, we dream about doing wonderful things when we grow up. Sometimes our hunger to achieve drives us into unrealistic expectations. We think we should win prizes for the best this or the best that, and if we don't, we feel we have failed. Our ideal of success is the brass ring on the carousel that continually eludes our grasp. Often, our merry-go-round of activity moves faster and faster, and we end up dizzy, with little sense of who we are apart from our accomplishments. Our inner selves get lost in never-ending circles of busyness.

When compulsive activity replaces compulsive eating, we may be slender but not serene. The Twelve Step program teaches us to re-examine our ideas of what constitutes success. We learn to measure success in terms of what we have shared and given away rather than in terms of the "things" we have collected for ourselves. The wisdom behind that criteria is simple: sharing and giving produce more satisfaction than collecting things or piling up achievements.

We understand this in bits and snatches, but then we may often forget. Wisdom and serenity get lost in frenetic activity that prevents us from taking the quiet time necessary to get to know ourselves and our Higher Power.

Compulsive shopping is a symptom of inner emptiness. While each new purchase gives us a temporary sense of happiness, it doesn't last. Like the high from a couple of drinks, it soon fades and we feel compelled to go out and buy something else. We fall into the trap of defining ourselves in terms of our possessions.

Switching from an obsession with food to an obsession with work, exercise, or any other activity indicates low self-esteem and inner emptiness. It's as though we're afraid of who we are or bored with who we are, or critical of who we are, or ignorant of who we are. We can't tolerate the idea of just "being," so we constantly have to be "doing."

When we don't like ourselves and are not at peace with our Higher Power, the brass ring is forever just out of reach. However much we do or achieve or collect, we're never satisfied.

What About Money?

Is there ever enough? Is money the magic substance? We may have heard that "a woman can never be too rich or too thin." (What about a man?) Do we believe that? Believing literally that one can never be too thin is the road to anorexia, which can result in death due to self-starvation. Believing you can never be too rich is equally dangerous. When the obsession with money becomes self-controlling, the result is emotional and spiritual starvation.

Achievement and success are often measured in monetary terms. We tend to equate money with security. A slang term for money is "bread," so here we are back to food!

Material needs, wants, and desires—we have them, of course. What's difficult is to separate our wants from our needs. Can we accept that our Higher Power gives us what we need but not necessarily what we want? Are we willing to live one day at a time on the premise that, apart from God there is no security, but each day there are opportunities?

At the end of every meeting, we pray that our Higher Power will "give us this day our daily bread." As the Steps begin providing direction for our lives, we can gradually loosen our grasp on material forms of security so that our hands are open to receive the spiritual gifts that satisfy.

Someday My Prince/Princess Will Come

Those of us with a history of using excess food to meet our dependency needs often use relationships in the same way. Going back to personal experience, I had fantasies from age eleven about the perfect relationship that would bring me happiness forever. It would make up for all the hurts I had ever suffered, and life was going to be a dream. The fantasy was fueled by dependency. Along with food, I got hooked on romance.

Something about fantasy makes us feel good, and so we persist in returning to the dream. Dreaming can be healthy; fantasies not only are pleasant, but they can also fire our imagination so that we try new things and expand our horizons. It is when fantasy prevents us from functioning in the here and now that we're in trouble. When fantasy combines with dependency, we may use it as an escape from the demands of a mature relationship. If reality doesn't measure up to our dreams, we try to change reality.

Here are some examples: We go from one romance to another, searching for the perfect lover. We try multiple sexual encounters, compulsively seeking an ultimate satisfaction we can't seem to find. Or perhaps we're just trying to prove to ourselves that we're attractive. We wander in and out of relationships looking for someone to take care of us and make us feel whole. Or we stay with one partner, but are chronically bored and dissatisfied because the person does not fulfill our dreams.

A friend of mine, Marcia T., told me that the only time her appetite was under control was when she was in love. When she wasn't in love she was obsessed with food and she went to O.A. When she was in love she was obsessed with her new friend, and she didn't go to O.A. because she "didn't have time and didn't need it."

The best-seller, *Women Who Love Too Much*, is relevant to men as well as women. If we expect another person to make us happy, we will be disappointed. Love is wonderful—romance, sex, passion, and tenderness are wonderful—relationships can be wonderful—but we become obsessed with them when we use them compulsively to avoid the growing we must do on our own.

Looking for a fantasy prince or princess to meet every desire prevents us from developing mature, satisfying relationships with real people. The "perfect stranger" remains just that until we get to know the person and come close enough to see the imperfections. Then, if our expectations are so unrealistic that we can't tolerate a less-than-perfect person, we start looking all over again for another "perfect stranger."

It's possible to get hooked on romance, relationships, or sex in the same way we get hooked on excess food, chemicals, or various compulsive activities. When we need more and more in terms of quantity, we often receive less and less in terms of satisfaction. I heard in one of the O.A. meeting rooms that compulsive eaters don't have love affairs, they take hostages. Back to Marcia T. Each time she got involved in a new romance, she believed that to please her man she had to do everything his way. She was terrified of being rejected and abandoned.

Each romance Marcia had, she found herself linked with a person who, for one reason or another, was incapable of giving her the love she needed. So she constantly felt frustrated and insecure. Since her last romance ended, Marcia has been back in O.A. for three months. She says she has some new insight into the way she acts and reacts, and she has promised herself that the next time she falls in love she's going to stay with the program. "I may do the same stupid thing all over again," Marcia says, sighing, "but if I stay plugged into the program and maintain contact with people I can talk to, I'll have a better chance of knowing that I'm doing the same stupid thing. I do need the program. If I get involved in a new relationship, I see now that, more than ever, I will still need my program."

The Real Thing

When an obsession becomes more painful than the pain we try to avoid, we are motivated to dump the obsession. The question is, what replaces it? Another obsession? To depend on substances or activities or other people to take care of us is to make them into Higher Powers of sorts, substitutes for the real thing.

In my experience, there is no substitute for spiritual growth. Although my concept of God may not be exactly the same as yours, I believe that the more fully we are able to trust and depend on a spiritual force to direct our lives, the stronger we become. We can't define God for each other, but we can share the results of working a spiritual program. The God of my understanding does not promise a pain-free existence. Perhaps that's why I tried so many substitutes. Somewhere, I thought there should be an easier way. But the substances and activities I thought would help me avoid pain did not come through for me. Sooner or later, pain caught up with me—the pain of a binge, a hangover, a series of broken relationships—and, ultimately, the original emotional pain I had wanted to escape was there too.

We're all going to have problems, however fortunate we may be. As long as we are alive, we are subject to fear, hurt, loneliness, shame, and anger. We can escape through dangerous dependencies or we can handle our difficulties by coming to believe in and rely on a Power greater than ourselves to get us through whatever comes along. When we accept that there will be problems and pain instead of trying to run away, we can find greater strength and understanding.

For me, learning to trust in a Higher Power means coming to depend on the real thing instead of on substitutes. I've tried managing my life by myself and that doesn't work. What works for me is turning my will and my life over to the care of God, praying only for knowledge of God's will for me and the power to carry that out. Never mind the substitutes. I want the real thing.

CHAPTER NINE

Catastrophic Coverage

Earthquake. Fire. Flood. Tornado. Divorce. Accidents. Bankruptcy. Losing a job. Problems with children. Problems with aging parents. Illness. Death of loved ones. How many of these crises have you faced?

Given the choice, we'd probably decide to skip the crisis and catastrophe department altogether. How much nicer and more pleasant our days and months and years would be if they glided smoothly along without a hint of disaster. Odds are, however, that none of us will escape having to deal with many of the above crises, plus a few more.

For protection we buy insurance. We have health and accident insurance, homeowners' policies, automobile insurance, disability and unemployment compensation, and life insurance. Our insurance policies can, to a degree, offset the financial burden of bad things that might happen to us. That's what catastrophic coverage is for. If fire damages the house, a homeowner's policy helps with the expense of repairing and restoring our property. If someone has a serious illness, health insurance covers part of the expenses.

We may be protected from financial disaster, but what about the emotional wear and tear of a crisis? How do we weather the storms of death, divorce, and problems with adolescent children and aging parents? Fortunately, there is help. Professional counseling and therapy, support groups, friends, and community resources are available.

What do you do, though, when you find yourself waking up at three o'clock morning after morning, anguishing over a problem and unable to go back to sleep? You can't call your therapist, and you're reluctant to disturb a friend or family member. That's where the program comes through for us: we can learn to make contact with a Higher Power through prayer and meditation. The Twelve Steps can show us the way to attaining greater strength than we had before the crisis.

Before the program, we used food to try to ward off trouble, to allay our fears, and to provide comfort when bad things happened. Most of us overate, some of us underate, and some of us binged and purged. Now we have a program. How does it come through for us when the going gets rough? How do we build the strength that will cover and support us in a catastrophe? What inner resources will see us through the death of loved ones and other losses?

Before and After: Monica's Story

Monica W., leading a meeting, talked about two of the most difficult times in her life. One was before she joined O.A. and the other was after:

"When my husband lost his job, I fell apart. We had moved three times in five years, and Ed was talking about moving again—back to Philadelphia. We had four children, ages twelve, ten, seven, and five. I hadn't worked since before the oldest was born.

"The idea of another move was more than I could face. I told Ed he could go, but the kids and I were staying here.

"I had been slowly putting on weight since Ed and I got married. When I started thinking about how we were going to make it with no money coming in, all I could do was eat. I knew I should go look for a job, but I was paralyzed with fear. And I was mad at Ed for not being a better provider.

"The summer he was out of work, I gained 30 pounds. I finally got a job at the end of August, and a week later Ed got a good offer from a company here in town.

"We had gone through most of our savings, and the marriage was at a very low ebb. I felt I couldn't depend on Ed, and he said I hadn't stood by him when he was having trouble. We fought almost every night and then I would binge. Sometimes I got up in the middle of the night to eat more. The next morning it would be hard to get to work. Some days I didn't make it, and after four weeks I quit the job.

"The pounds kept coming on, even though Ed's crisis was over. He said I was getting fat just because I knew it turned him off. One of the girls at work had told me about O.A. I didn't think it would help, but I had to do something so I decided to try.

"That was seven years ago. I didn't get abstinent for nearly six months, yet something kept me going back to meetings. It was a couple of years before the weight came off. But many changes were taking place.

"To give you an idea of what a different person I was after five years in the program, I'll tell you about the second most difficult period in my life. That was when we found out that Alec, our oldest boy and seventeen at the time, was addicted to drugs.

"Before O.A., I would have blamed Ed and proceeded to fall apart again. Thanks to the program, though, I was able to move away from useless attempts to find someone to blame. I tried to work with Ed and the whole family to see how we could get Alec the help he needed. We got him into a treatment program that included family sessions. Ed and I went to Al-Anon meetings too.

"It was touch and go for about a year. The amazing thing was that I didn't turn to food. And Ed and I didn't fight with each other about whose fault it was. Alec's problem actually brought us closer together. Through Al-Anon, Ed got into the Steps with me.

"I didn't go back to food and I didn't fall apart. I maintained my abstinence, and I kept working full time at the new job I got about a year after joining O.A. Alec's now in college. I still worry about him—he's had a couple of slips—but I get better because I know a Higher Power is taking care of us.

"If the problems with Alec had happened before I got into the program, I don't know what I would have done. I'm so grateful to be recovering—our whole family is recovering."

Breaking Up

"When Peggy said she was leaving, I couldn't believe it," says Dan R., a newcomer to our Thursday night group. He has been in A.A. for several years and in O.A. for eight months. He says:

"I was stunned. Peggy had put up with my drinking for nearly twelve years. Finally, I got sober, and then the problem was food. Peggy was the one who encouraged me to go to O.A. She was a big help; she fixed meals according to my food plan and didn't mind that I went to meetings at night. Then, when at long last I seemed to be getting my act together, she ups and leaves!

"I'm still in a state of shock. I don't believe it's happened. I don't want to believe it. Sixteen years of marriage down the drain."

For many weeks, our Thursday night group shared with Dan his anguish, anger, bitterness, and all the other emotions that a break-up causes. Slowly, we saw him work through a mountain of confusion and despair and come out on the other side.

"I still don't fully understand what happened," says Dan, a year after the break-up. "I've done a lot of thinking and reading and praying this last year, and it still seems crazy, but I have more insight now. For one thing, there's the issue of codependency. As long as I was down and out, Peggy was my rescuer. Then when I began to get well, the dynamics of the relationship changed. Was it because I didn't need a caretaker anymore and Peggy was out of a job? I don't know."

After his wife left, Dan suffered from severe depression. He felt isolated and abandoned. "I can't tell you how many times I was ready to start drinking again. The way I looked at it, what did I have to lose that I hadn't already lost?

"For months, I went to a meeting every night, either A.A. or O.A. That's what saved me. Otherwise I would have gone back to the booze and the food.

"I didn't take a drink. I did slip with food a few times but I got back. I don't see how anybody gets through a divorce without the kind of friends I've found in the Twelve Step programs."

Hard as this last year has been for Dan, he considers it one of his most important for personal growth. "I'm not the same guy Peggy walked out on," he says. "I went through hell, but I came out the other end. With no booze, no food binges, and no wife, I had to sit down and face myself and find out who I was. I couldn't duck the issues any longer."

Dan explains that he had always felt like a failure. "Whatever I did, it was never good enough for my mother. I'm sure one of the reasons I married Peg was that she was the sort of person my mother admired—smart, ambitious, and with social savvy. If someone like Peg would be my wife, I thought I must be okay, but then when she left that proved I had been a failure all along.

"Sometimes when I awakened in the middle of the night full of anxiety and depression, I'd read a while from one of the meditation books I kept by my bed. Then I said the Serenity Prayer. I turned my worries over to God. Gradually, I began to sleep more and worry less.

"I did a Fourth Step, which focused heavily on my relationship with Peggy. The more honest I was about my part in our problems, the more I was able to let go of some of the bitterness, anger, and resentment I felt toward her.

"Even though Peg knows about the Twelve Step program, I don't think she really understood what I was trying to do with Step Nine. When we spoke, she kept asking me what I wanted from her. I was very careful not to make accusations, just to talk about the mistakes I had made and how I had contributed to our botched-up relationship. I was able to say I was sorry.

"Step Nine was the turning point for me in being able to accept the fact that, whether I liked it or not, my marriage was over. My attempt to make amends may not have been so great, but it sure did great things for me! I don't hate Peggy anymore, and I don't feel like a failure. My fears are much less intense. My life is in God's hands. As long as I stick close to the program, I'll be okay."

Powerless Over Death

My grandfather used to say, "Everything has an end except a sausage and that has two." That statement was not funny to me; it was chilling, deeply frightening. I didn't like to think of endings when I was a little girl—not the end of an ice cream cone, not the end of a party, not the end of a life, especially not the end of my life or my parents' lives.

But it is impossible to avoid thinking about endings. Recently, my eighty-six-year-old mother was hospitalized for ten days and then moved to a nursing home. My father, who lives by himself and is in poor health, is also eighty-six. A close friend of mine died a few months ago, leaving a husband and four children who are under age fifteen. Another friend has just learned that he has cancer.

Our natural inclination is to deny the reality of death, but sooner or later it hits home. Then what do we do?

In trying to deal with death's reality, I have reached for help through the Twelve Steps. In the face of death, we are ultimately powerless. We will each die. The only questions are where and when and how. Accepting that we are powerless over death, ours or someone else's, is not easy. Every fiber of our being protests the loss of a loved one. When they are obviously suffering it becomes easier to say good-bye, but only slightly. Our natural impulse is to "rage, rage against the dying of the light."[1]

I think the acceptance of death is a giant step, perhaps the biggest one we'll ever take on our journey to emotional and spiritual maturity. With this acceptance, life becomes more precious. Our days will not go on forever. Those we love will not always be with us. Each moment and each day which we are given becomes supremely valuable. The philosophy of one day at a time is our response to the knowledge that our existence is finite. Since I shall not live forever, I will live today to its fullest.

When viewed in this way, admitting and accepting our powerlessness over death might help us to acknowledge a Power greater than ourselves. Here we move to Step Two. Coming to believe in a Higher Power rescues us from the insanity of thinking we can or should be able to control life and death.

My mother and father will die. I shall die. My children will die. I decide many times each day to give God my life and their lives. And then I understand that all of our lives have been in the hands of God all along. I am now at Step Three, praying for the knowledge of my Higher Power's will for me today. How can I help those who are dying? How can I contribute to the living? We are all living and dying every day.

Because I will not live forever, I need to, in a figurative sense, take stock periodically and clean house when necessary, so that my days will be productive and fulfilling and enjoyable. This leads to Step Four, taking a searching and fearless moral inventory. I can be fearless now because I have confronted the inevitability of death. God is in charge. There is nothing more to fear.

Next come Steps Five, Six, and Seven. We share the frustrations over what we cannot do, and the satisfactions from the progress we are making, especially in spiritual growth. We are willing to be free of the character defects that get in our way, and ask God to remove them.

We make amends now. Now, today, is when we can do all in our power to heal a broken relationship, to speak words of appreciation and love that we may not be able to say tomorrow. Do we assume that those we love know we love them? Are we afraid of being vulnerable if we tell them out loud? We may not have another chance.

If we live each day to its fullest, we will keep our emotional and spiritual house in order. What would you do with today if you knew there would be no tomorrow? Continuing to take personal inventory and promptly admitting mistakes leaves us with a clean slate each day.

The knowledge of death can propel us to reach out for something spiritual, something ongoing and eternal. Without the support of a Higher Power, confronting the void of an ultimate ending is a terrifying prospect for me. Step Eleven obtains for us a new kind of life insurance policy, one that we start collecting on immediately. The closer we come to the knowledge of God's will for us, and the more fully we are able to carry that out, the richer each day becomes for us and the less frightened we are of death.

Some of us believe in life after death; some of us do not. Those of us committed to the Twelve Steps experience, in various ways, what we call a spiritual awakening. For some, this is a forecast of a spiritual life to come. For others, it is enough to experience a new dimension of life just for today. Either way, we can share what we have with those around us, bringing the peace and serenity we gain through the program to those whose lives we touch.

Paradoxically, without death there could be no life. We are born, we grow old, we die and make room for new life. Acceptance of death frees us from anxiety and denial so we can live fully now, in the present, every moment.

Where's the Safety Net?

We cannot arrange the events in our lives so that there will be a no-catastrophe guarantee. We are much more likely to have troubles than to escape them. The crucial factor is how we deal with difficult events in our lives, foreseen and unforeseen.

In my morning newspaper today, a report of an air disaster told that more than 150 passengers were presumed dead. On another page, a new book was reviewed that predicts a major depression within three years.

What do we do when disaster strikes? Do we fall apart? Do we try to blot out our sorrow with excess food or alcohol? How can we get on with the business of living, of rebuilding a house after a fire, a child's health after an illness or accident, our own lives after a divorce or the death of a spouse?

Those of us who have turned to the Twelve Step program out of our weakness, our inability to handle food in a normal way, have been blessed with a source of strength that we can apply to all of the other difficulties we encounter. In this sense, the program is our safety net.

When disaster strikes and we lose our equilibrium, we have a structure that will support us. Monica used it when her oldest son developed a drug problem. Dan used it to grow through the trauma of divorce. Millions of Twelve Steppers have found the program to be a way of coping successfully with every trial and tribulation that comes along. Although we're not immune from disaster, we have tools to see us through.

Our safety net does more than simply protect us from coming apart at the seams under the stress of a traumatic situation. It helps us to continually grow and develop so that we come out of the crisis stronger than ever. But to make progress, we must first accept where we are now. The loss of property, the illness, the broken relationship, the death of someone close, even our eventual death must be accepted before we move on to greater strength. With guidance by and support from a Power greater than ourselves, we may gain new life and growth out of our pain. Continuing to practice the principles of our program is the key.

CHAPTER TEN

Is This All There Is?

Never enough. When we were bingeing, we never got enough food. However many compulsive bites we took, satisfaction always beckoned just ahead, in the next bite, and the next, and the next. As overeaters, we ate until we had consumed too much, and too much was never enough.

Wearing a size eight, graduating from college, getting a new job, getting married, buying a house, having children, getting divorced, getting another job, buying a new car, getting married again, taking a trip—is it ever enough?

Working the program, taking the Steps, becoming abstinent, going to meetings, making phone calls, writing a food plan, working the program, going to more meetings—is this all there is?

Carla N. is a recovering compulsive eater. She describes a turning point in her recovery that occurred while her mother was visiting her.

"Neil and I had just bought our first house. We had spent more than a year trying to find a place we could afford, in a decent neighborhood with enough space for ourselves and our two children. The longer it took to get the money together, the more the price of houses increased. But we finally found something we could afford—just barely. We moved in June, and my mother came to visit during the first week of August.

"I don't think I'll ever forget the last night my mother was with us. It was a very bad scene. All week Mother had been critical, which was nothing new, but it was definitely getting to me. Neil was away on a business trip, so it was just Mother, the children, and myself. According to Mother, everything was wrong with the house. Jack and Vicki didn't have a large enough yard to play in; the west sun made the kitchen too hot; the rooms were awkwardly arranged; the basement smelled musty; the walls were too thin, and so forth.

"I was trying to survive the week without getting into the kind of fight my mother and I always seem to have when we're together for more than two days. I didn't make it. After Jack and Vicki were in bed, mother made a remark about what a noisy neighborhood it was, and I exploded. I told her she'd spent the week criticizing me and the house and Neil and the children.

"Later, I went back into the living room to say I was sorry and found my mother sobbing on the sofa. Before I could say anything, she cried out in anguish, 'We wanted so much more for you!'

"These words have reverberated in my head ever since. They have become a theme song for my problems with food. After Mother had left, I began to see how crazy it all was. Here was Mother, sobbing over the 'tragedy' of my life. I had a good husband, two cute kids, a house in the suburbs, a station wagon, friends, a dog, a good-paying part-time job—and Mother wanted more. I wanted more. Nothing was ever enough. I saw that, for me, food was a symbol of all the things I wanted and didn't have. And no matter how much I did have—food or things—I always wanted more."

Half Empty or Half Full?

How do you look at the pluses and minuses of your day-to-day situation? Do you tend to see the cup as half empty or as half full? If we look for negatives, we will find them. The opposite is also true: if we look for the positives in any given situation, we will find those too. The choice is ours. Will we choose to focus on what we don't have or what we do have?

An attitude of chronic discontent may be rooted in unrealistic expectations. Carla N. said she grew up planning to marry someone with lots of money. That was her mother's plan for her too. She fell in love with Neil when she was 20. He didn't have lots of money, but he had everything else that Carla thought she wanted in a husband.

"I love Neil. We have much more than most of the people in this world. Before I got into the O.A. program, though, all I could think about was what we didn't have. My teenage dream of what life would be like when I was 30 included a big house with a swimming pool, a maid, a couple of fancy cars, European vacations, the whole bit.

"I see that now for what it was: a fantasy. I work part-time as a nurse in a big city hospital. When I look at the people who come in who are not only very sick but also very poor, I appreciate how much Neil and I and the children have.

"You know, the more grateful I am for what we do have, the less I'm tempted to binge. I know my bingeing was a way of trying to compensate for what I thought was missing in my life."

What are your expectations? Are they realistic? Do fantasies about what might be make you dissatisfied with what is? Do you expect abstinence to solve all of your problems? Counting blessings instead of sheep may sound trite, but it works!

Along with counting our blessings each day and being grateful for what we have, we also need to give ourselves credit for the things we have done right. Our daily inventories should not be limited to the mistakes we have made.

Unrealistic expectations may cause us to see our cup as half empty instead of half full. Too much time spent in fantasy spoils us for reality. Another reason that our cup may seem only half full could be that we drain it too fast, without taking time to savor its contents.

As compulsive eaters and bingers, most of us are familiar with eating quickly. It may be that a voice inside of us is telling us to stop, or we may fear someone coming in and finding us bingeing. Whatever the reason, fast eating is not good for us physically or psychologically. When we voraciously wolf down our food, we don't get the message that we have had enough. The amount doesn't seem like enough, because the experience of eating is over so quickly. Our bodies don't have time to signal our brains that enough has been consumed. Since we don't feel satiated, we keep eating more and faster.

So, too, the cup of our life experience seems empty if we drain it too quickly without pausing to savor the ordinary, everyday events and blessings. If we are constantly looking ahead to a better job, more money, or a new relationship, we never feel as though we have much of anything of value. But at any given moment, a multitude of sensations are within range of our awareness.

What do you see now if you raise your head and look around? What do you hear? What can you touch, and how does it feel?

"When I was in the hospital," said my friend who has cancer, "I was lucky enough to have my bed next to a window. Just being able to wake up and look out and see the leaves and branches of a tree moving against the sky was a treat. The changes from light to dark, the clouds, the colors of the sunset, once in a while a bird—my window framed an ever-evolving panorama."

If we don't take time to enjoy what we have, then what we have will never be enough. I remember in one of my favorite children's books a line from a Robert Louis Stevenson poem: "The world is so full of a number of things, I'm sure we should all be happy as kings."[1] We should be, but not many of us are. We are geared toward consumption. The message we get from media advertising is that to enjoy, we must buy. We watch the soap operas and sitcoms where the furnishings and clothes are new and elegant. And we sigh, thinking this is the way folks ought to live.

Today Is Ours

When we wake up each morning, we have a choice. We can think about the day's down side (it's raining, we have a dental appointment) or we can focus on good things (the garden

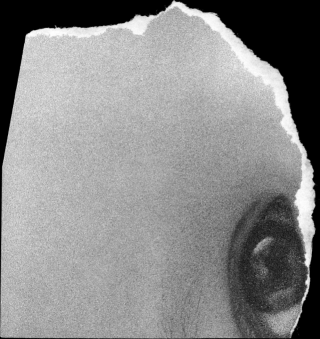

needs rain, we plan a long phone conversation with a friend).

Before the program, my today was a very thin slice sandwiched between two very thick hunks of yesterday and tomorrow. I alternated between either following a rigid schedule or rebelling and doing relatively nothing except bingeing. Most of today was lost, because I spent so much time being preoccupied with past and future. I constantly tried to determine what I was "supposed" to be doing, but I lacked an inner sense of direction. Should I go to graduate school? Get a job? Join a garden club? Paint the living room? I thought whatever I chose meant that I was missing out on something else. And how did I know whether I had picked the right course of action? What terrible thing might happen to me next year that I could perhaps prevent if I did something else now?

All of these considerations created anxiety, and the only way I knew to relieve it was to eat or take a pill or drink alcohol. Then I had more to be anxious about: my lack of control, my expanding girth, and my increasing dependence on chemicals.

The concept of "just for today" has changed my life. When I focused on yesterday and tomorrow, today seemed insignificant, dull, and boring. What was real shrank and got lost in what had been or what might be. "Just for today" clears the dust and debris of the past and the unknown challenges of the future so that today can sparkle. A Zen saying suggests that "only in a hut built for the moment can one live without fear."[2] It is by living in the present, just for today, that I am liberated from resentment and worry—resentment about what I didn't have yesterday and worry about what I might not have tomorrow. When today is no longer compressed by the past and the future, it expands to hold all of the interesting events and feelings in my world now. Sure, I do what I can to make amends for past mistakes and to prevent future problems. But then I let go of both so that I can enjoy now.

Since I can only try to know God's will for me now, today, I am not in such a quandary about what I "should" be doing.

Since the program teaches me to leave results to God, all I must be concerned with is following the inner direction I receive each day.

I find that when I am fully aware of what is happening to me, I am not bored. My everyday routine only becomes boring when I start wishing I were somewhere else and begin tuning out my real situation. For today to be mine, I must claim it and concentrate on its details. Today is unique. I will never have the same 24 hours again.

Today is ours when we accept it as a gift from a Higher Power. We did not create this day. We do not have control over its shape and content any more than we can determine whether it will be cloudy or sunny. How we think and act will, however, have a profound effect on how we experience today.

Abstinence Is Not Enough

Abstinence from compulsive eating is the cornerstone of our freedom to live fully, one day at a time, and to react positively to situations that arise. As a result of bingeing, we felt negative and depressed; it was difficult to see the good side of anything. Our outlook may begin improving when, new to the O.A. program, we concentrate on becoming abstinent. It is the entrance to our new life. But abstinence by itself is not enough.

Our program offers so much more. There's more than just not bingeing or not being obsessed with food and diets. Abstinence is an open door leading to new adventure, a greater capacity for intimacy, and the potential for spiritual growth.

If all we had to look forward to each day was eating three moderate meals with nothing in between, it's not likely that many of us would stay with the program for long. We need something positive to take the place of our obsession with food and diets. This comes, as we keep coming back to the fellowship.

Listen to how it worked for Fran G.:

"I dropped out of the program after a couple of years. I got tired of meetings, tired of food plans, tired of the same old stuff. I figured I could do it on my own. Well, I couldn't. It took me a year to find that out, though, and by the end of that year I had gained back all the weight I had lost, plus about 25 more pounds.

"Even worse than the weight gain was the pit of depression I sunk into. It was like being at the bottom of a deep hole with no way out.

"An O.A. friend of mine kept calling me about once a month to see how I was doing, and each month I got worse. Donna kept suggesting that I ought to get back to a meeting, but I couldn't stand the thought of gritting my teeth and trying to follow a food plan again.

"Finally Donna said, 'Look, why don't you just come and listen tomorrow night. What else have you got to do?' Well, all I had to do was watch television and eat, so to get her off my back I said I'd go, but just to that one meeting. No way was I going to get back into the program.

"It's amazing I could hurt so bad and still be so stubborn. But I looked at the program as something that restricted my freedom, something that told me to do things I didn't like, such as write a food plan, and to not do things I did like, such as eat donuts in the afternoon. I figured I had tried the program and it just didn't work for me.

"Anyway, I went to the meeting with Donna. I felt really embarrassed to be there looking the way I did, since some of the folks there knew me from when I had been in the program. They were obviously doing well, and I obviously wasn't.

"I was feeling really sorry for myself and not listening to what was being read, until suddenly some words jumped out at me—the part about no human power being able to relieve our obsession, but that 'God could and would if He were sought.'

"Then I had this terrific insight that, yes I had white-knuckled it through abstinence for over a couple of years, but I hadn't sought God.

"I hadn't paid much attention to the Steps. I figured the

main thing was to lose the weight. Well, I was able to lose 40 pounds, but I never did stop being obsessed with food. I didn't really take Step One until that night at the meeting with Donna, when I finally understood there was no way I was going to get rid of the obsession by myself. 'God could and would if He were sought.' I thought about that for the rest of the evening, and when I went to bed I had a little talk with my Higher Power. 'Okay, God,' I said. 'Take it away. I can't.'

"I didn't make a food plan the next day, but I did seek God. I got out my "Twelve and Twelve"* and started reading. All day, whenever I felt like going after the food, I asked God to remove the obsession. I didn't binge."

Fran came back and started again. This time her top priority was her relationship with a Higher Power. "I wasn't big on the God stuff before," says Fran, "but my way hadn't worked. I guess I had what you might call a spiritual awakening. Abstinence happened in a very natural sort of way. I concentrated on staying in touch with my Higher Power, and the abstinence seemed to take care of itself.

"The type of abstinence I had before was boring. Now there is a good kind of excitement in my life. I get new ideas every day. I've started taking dance lessons—something I've always wanted to do. And I play tennis at least three times a week. In the fall, I'm returning to school to get a degree in counseling.

"Food is wonderful, but it's no longer the be-all and end-all of my existence. I'm not obsessed with it. God comes first."

Today Is Enough

Those of us who have been obsessed with food, diets, and weight are in for a treat when we work the program and the

---

*The "Twelve and Twelve" is the *Twelve Steps and Twelve Traditions*, published by Alcoholics Anonymous World Services, Inc., New York, N.Y.

obsession is lifted. We can begin to live "normal" lives. We have so many new possibilities. The beauty of our program is that it gives us a blueprint for continued spiritual growth and expansion.

How we put together our new lives is up to each of us individually, one day at a time. For me, the challenge is to deal to the best of my ability with the issues that come along each day. I don't want to expect too much, nor do I want to be satisfied with too little. Like Fran, I think my Higher Power is the key to avoiding both extremes.

Nelson W., a friend, remembers that his mother would urge him to eat when he wasn't really hungry, on the grounds that he might be hungry later. He says he never knew what it was like to feel hungry, because his mother's "prevention campaign," which he adopted as his own, was so effective. The disadvantage was that Nelson was overweight from infancy. He never knew how much was enough until he hit middle age and found the Twelve Step program. Nelson says he's gradually learning to trust that enough food will be available when he needs it. He knows how it feels to be hungry, and he knows what it is to have enough.

Is this all there is? We ask this question when our expectations are unrealistically high, when we don't pay attention to what we have and savor it, and when we try to get along without a Higher Power. I believe we are put together in such a way as to be unsatisfied until we give our spiritual selves room to grow. When we let a Higher Power take priority, we begin to trust that we will have what we need—when we need it. When we're growing spiritually, today is enough.

CHAPTER ELEVEN

Yes, There Is Life
After Abstinence

One morning I got up half an hour early so I could leave my suburban house at 6:30, thus getting a jump on the rush-hour traffic. I needed to be at work in the city by 7:15 to prepare for a meeting.

But at 6:45 I came to a standstill on the parkway in a traffic back up. I could see police flares ahead. I turned on my car radio and learned there had been a very serious accident, closing the parkway in both directions.

In front of me, numerous cars were turning around and heading back the other way. The remainder were being slowly diverted to a small side road that led to an alternate route. I knew the route would be jammed for at least an hour.

Rather than take my place in the creeping caravan, I decided I would be better off pulling into a nearby gas station, not far from the police flares, and waiting for the parkway to reopen. I couldn't believe that at least one lane of traffic would not be allowed to move through before long. I gambled that my way would involve only a few minutes' delay.

Well, the flares remained in place as I watched the slow-moving line of cars inch its way toward the alternate route. They were moving and I was not.

More and more vehicles took the alternate route. When I had been sitting at the gas station for about half an hour, I decided to reassess the situation. I left my car, walked to where the policemen were standing, and asked how much longer it might be before we could get through.

"Oh, another hour at least," was the reply.

What did I do? I got in line to take the alternate route. It took me 2 hours to get to work instead of the normal 45 minutes. I arrived at 8:30.

I've been thinking about that experience, comparing my reactions to it with those I might have had before abstinence.

Before abstinence, I also tried shortcuts that ended up taking longer. Before abstinence, I also tended to do things my way and was reluctant to ask questions that might have elicited useful information. Before abstinence, I also indulged in wishful, "magical" thinking.

Those are some similarities. Now for the differences.

First, I didn't panic when I discovered I was in the middle of a major traffic jam on a morning when I needed to be at work early. I didn't rant and rave. I accepted the situation. One of the first thoughts that crossed my mind was what a co-worker had said to me recently. "When I get delayed because of an accident, I'm just glad I wasn't in the accident." I was grateful. If I had been coming down the parkway earlier, it could have been me.

Before abstinence, I would have fumed and fretted; my best-laid plans had been foiled. This time I didn't do that. Having paperwork with me, I passed the time at the gas station constructively. The situation was out of my hands, and I knew I could only be responsible for my reaction to it.

Second, I accepted that I might, in trying to save time, have made the wrong choice. Why did I think I should go it alone instead of asking for help? Why didn't I ask the police sooner? Why did I think something was going to happen just because I wished it would? Good questions. I'm working on them.

Before abstinence, I would have been hard on myself for being so stupid. If I had gone with the detour at the beginning, instead of coming up with a "better idea," I would have saved a half hour. But I didn't chastise myself. I accepted that I was slow to ask for information, that I had not made the best choice. I realized I was doing the best I could at the time. I thought, *next time maybe I'll do better.*

Let's look at the bigger picture: I got to work, having accomplished some paperwork for my meeting while I was waiting. The sky did not fall because my schedule was delayed. Before abstinence, my day would have been off to a very rocky start, if not shot to pieces because of that one incident. This time I was emotionally serene.

One more important difference: I had a brown-bag lunch with me in the car. Before abstinence, I would have eaten it while sitting at the gas station. When I got to work and carried the bag into the office, I realized I hadn't given food a thought!

The Promises

Yes, there is life after abstinence. There are traffic jams and leaky basements and broken engagements. And there is serenity. And joy. The Big Book, *Alcoholics Anonymous*, puts it this way:

> We are going to know a new freedom and a new happiness. We will not regret the past nor wish to shut the door on it. We will comprehend the word serenity and we will know peace. No matter how far down the scale we have gone, we will see how our experience can benefit others. That feeling of uselessness and self-pity will disappear. We will lose interest in selfish things and gain interest in our fellows. Self-seeking will slip away. Our whole attitude and outlook upon life will change. Fear of people and of economic insecurity will leave us. We will intuitively know how to handle situations which used to baffle us. We will suddenly realize that God is doing for us what we could not do for ourselves.[1]

Are these extravagant promises? We think not. They are being fulfilled among us—sometimes quickly, sometimes slowly. They will always materialize if we work for them.

These promises, according to the Big Book, will happen if we are "painstaking" about working the Steps. When I first heard these promises, part of me thought they were too good to be true. Another part of me, though, felt a glimmer of hope and a thrill of possibility. And for twelve years, these promises have been coming true for me—sometimes slowly, sometimes quickly.

Like Fran in the previous chapter, I have been taking dancing lessons. Once a week, I go to a class in a studio with mirrors. At times I catch sight of myself and think, *This can't be me. I must have died and gone to heaven.*

Seeing myself in the mirror looking the way I want to look is only part of it. Yes, I'm slender, and I like that very, very much. But even nicer is the way I feel. I'm moving to music, something I love to do. I'm learning, I'm getting better, I'm willing to make mistakes and try again. I don't have a steady partner now, and that's okay. I have good friends.

Not long ago, I visited my daughter in her new student living quarters. On one of the walls, she has photographs of her father and his new wife. I had a very hard time looking at those pictures last year, but this year that's okay too.

Twelve years ago, if anyone had told me where I would be today—physically, emotionally, psychologically, and spiritually—I would have been afraid to believe it. Although the change and growth have not come without pain, the results are more than worth the discomfort. "No pain, no gain," as we say in O.A. This program has given structure to what for me was once confusion. I may not always feel peace and serenity, but I know now where they are to be found.

We know that, for the Twelve Step promises to come true, we must work the program. The specifics of how we do it are up to each individual. But persistence pays. The more meetings we go to, the more we hear, the more we read—the more firmly the program sinks into our thoughts, feelings, and behavior. We take what we're ready for at the time, process it, and then come back for more.

Most of us felt some degree of isolation as our eating disorder progressed. As food took over our lives, we became increasingly out of touch with other people, our Higher Power, and even ourselves. Recovery puts us back in touch with those around us. For me, the sharing and caring I have found in the meeting rooms has spilled over into all of my relationships.

I came into the program thinking I had a problem with food, and I discovered I had a problem with living. I wanted to run the show, to have the events of each day go according to my wishes, and I was full of anxiety, possibly because something told me that was not likely to work. I discovered I could not maintain my abstinence unless I was willing to have the rest of my life completely overhauled. Life after abstinence is a good life. It may not be exactly what you or I expect—we are no longer calling the shots. We have to be willing to stop trying to run the show and agree to let a Higher Power take charge. That's the beauty of it all.

This is where the promised serenity and peace begin to surface. If all things come to us from the God of our understanding, then whatever happens to me today is what is supposed to occur. The people I encounter are in my life today for a reason. The events that happen are for my growth.

Since I am no longer obsessed with food, I have time and energy to enjoy people and events. I can do my job and contribute something useful. I can learn and share and feel and appreciate. Abstinence from compulsive eating sets me free to sample the abundance of all that life has to offer.

Again, here are some of the promises that appear in the Big Book:

Fear of people and of economic insecurity will leave us. Both of these have been big items for me. I won't say that my fear of either people or of economic insecurity has completely left, but each has abated considerably. I know that the less I think I need to impress other people, the less fear I have of them. I know that the more I focus on the reality that I have everything I need for today, the less I worry about future financial disaster. Abstinence and faith in a Higher Power are my fortresses against fear.

We will intuitively know how to handle situations which used to baffle us. I used to spend energy contriving devious ways to manipulate other people. Then I'd make up excuses so I wouldn't hurt their feelings or become the object of their anger. If relationships got tense, I retreated to food. I was always afraid I would say or do the wrong thing. Why is it that life is so much more comfortable for me now? I think it has to do, first, with getting straight with my Higher Power. Then, the honesty the program requires enhances all relationships. Since God is in charge I don't need to try to manipulate. I can relax, be spontaneous, and trust that the outcome will be good.

We will suddenly realize that God is doing for us what we could not do for ourselves. Some ego reduction is required to succeed in the program, but how lovely it is when we get there. God can and will do an infinitely better job of managing my life. Letting God do for me what I can't do myself is like jumping from an airplane into space, relying on the support of a Power greater than myself. The first trials I made at letting go and letting God were frightening, but good results increased my confidence.

The realization comes when we look around and see things falling into place in a way we may never have dreamed possible. The door we thought we wanted to open may have been firmly locked in front of us. And then we see another door standing ajar, leading to something much better than what we thought we wanted.

Walking the Walk

Ellen B.'s life after abstinence is a journey she takes one step at a time. Says Ellen B.:

"The direction of my life has changed. Instead of going downhill, I'm moving out of the mess I was in and walking on a path I never thought I'd find.

"I always had a weight problem, but it didn't get out of control until after I got married. Whenever I got mad at Ron, I'd eat. Whenever he hurt my feelings, I'd eat. Over three years, our relationship got worse and worse. We weren't communicating, our sex life deteriorated, I found fault with everything he did, but I rarely told him out loud what was bothering me or what I didn't like.

"I had a 'Hollywood' idea of how marriage was going to be. I was determined that Ron and I were going to be the perfect couple. When he did something I didn't like, I'd be swamped with critical feelings toward him, but I'd try to drop little hints and hope he'd get the message. When he didn't, I'd eat.

"If I hadn't found O.A. when I did, I don't think our relationship would have lasted more than another year or so. When I began to get honest with myself, I got honest with Ron too. But for a while, it was really rough—we didn't even like each other, never mind love.

"I had a choice. I could eat to compensate for my frustration and get fatter, or I could be honest about my needs and feelings and try to work out a way to take care of them.

"I'm getting better now at telling Ron what's bugging me without sounding like I'm attacking him. Doing my Fourth Step helped. We've had some wild arguments, but at least we're up front with each other. Honesty gets the conflicts out in the open where we've got a better chance of handling them."

Ellen says abstinence is her top priority now. "The weight is coming off, but important as that is, abstinence is more important. I don't look very far ahead or I get scared. I really don't see abstinence as a restriction. It's opened a whole new world for me. I'm a lot more spontaneous now that I don't shut down my feelings.

"I'm learning new things each day about Ron and myself, about activities we can share. Before I became abstinent, we were doing less and less together. Ron would go off fishing or sailing or biking, and I'd stay home and eat. Now I feel like being more active and doing things outdoors. I've sold Ron on other kinds of activities, too, such as going to museums and concerts. We're making new friends. We're communicating more and we're more intimate with each other.

"I still get my feelings hurt. I get mad. I get tired. I get depressed. I usually know when I need to go to a meeting, and if I don't know it myself, Ron is very likely to let me know! If I can't get to a meeting, I can always pick up the telephone and call someone. My program gets me into action. I know I have to keep moving or it won't work. I have to keep going to meetings, making phone calls, and working the Steps.

"I have so many more friends than I had before. Doing something for somebody else usually gets me out of a bad mood.

"It took a long time for me to come to terms with the idea of a Higher Power, but now I can't see any other explanation for the good things that have come my way."

Yes, there is life after abstinence. We come out of the food fog and discover that—surprise—everything is real. That goes for pain as well as for pleasure, but we now have tools for dealing with both. Life after abstinence is a richer, fuller, more abundant life than what we knew before. It's not easy, but it's better in so many ways than anything we may have dreamed possible. Walking the new path is a daily adventure, and when occasionally we stop to look back, we are usually amazed at how far we've come.

CHAPTER TWELVE

There Is No Finish Line

Everything is real! The fantasies and the fairy godmothers disappear in the light of abstinence and the Twelve Steps. We are left with the real world, where there is no finish line. We're doing what we do, one day at a time.

Along the way, there are milestones—a promotion, an engagement, a graduation ceremony. From the Twelve Step program, however, we do not graduate. That's because as long as we're breathing, we don't graduate from life, and the program is what equips us to enjoy all of the richness that life has to offer.

There will always be changes. That's what keeps the journey interesting. The program gives us a structure so that we can go through transitions without getting lost. Since we have turned our will and our lives over to a Higher Power, we can trust that wherever we are at any given moment is where we're supposed to be. We can let go and be carried along in the stream of goodness, moving for the sheer pleasure of being in motion rather than compulsively straining to reach a predetermined destination.

Maintenance: An Ongoing Process

Diets have beginnings and endings. A diet ends when you have lost a specified number of pounds and reached your goal weight, or when you have blown the diet so many times that you throw up your hands, fling your calorie counter out the window, and quit.

Abstinence and the program become a way of life. Instead

of going out with a bang or a whimper, they get stronger the longer you practice them. If you slip, you come back. If you don't slip, you come back too.

So there is no finish line. "But," you might ask, "what about when I do reach my goal weight? How do I make adjustments in my food plan? I don't want to keep losing weight." Or, if your problem was anorexia, you might say, "Now that I've gained the pounds I need, how do I avoid gaining more?"

One of the reasons we keep coming back is to get help with maintenance. This is not the time to stop working with a food sponsor, especially a sponsor who has had some experience with maintaining normal weight and continuing abstinence through the program. Somewhere, lurking in the back of our minds, we may still have the notion that once the weight is lost, we can go back to "normal" eating. But for those of us who are hard-core compulsive eaters, "normal" is "abnormal," because we were accustomed to unusually large amounts of food. A sponsor (along with our doctor) can help us determine our actual needs.

For those of us who suffered anorexia, "normal" was "abnormal," because we were accustomed to having not enough food. Again, a sponsor (along with our doctor) can help us determine our actual needs.

An important guideline for me in maintenance is to "keep it simple." I use a basic food plan that meets my nutritional needs; this includes foods that are quick and easy to prepare. I don't like to spend much time and energy thinking about food, buying it, or preparing it. My grocery list is much the same week after week. This may sound boring, but it works for me. I no longer use food for entertainment—I've found better things to do!

When it comes to making additions, we should proceed with caution. When my sponsor and I decided I needed more food, the first meal I increased was breakfast. That gave me additional calories early in the day so I could burn them for energy. It also was a time when I was least likely to consider bingeing.

"You mean I still have to think about food plans, forever and ever?" you may ask. After twelve years, I still think about food plans, but just for today. I don't think about them as often as I used to, because just as abstinence has become a habit, so has maintenance. I know what my body needs, and over the years in the program my appetite has adjusted to those needs. Before, I was trying to do it the other way around—adjust my needs to my appetite—and that was a disaster, since the more I fed my appetite, the more it expanded.

We each develop a food plan based on our nutritional needs and our lifestyle. I can tell you what works for me, but please remember that your needs should be determined by you, your doctor, and your sponsor. At this point in my recovery, I may not know at the beginning of the day exactly what I will have for each of my three meals, since my program is less rigid now than it was earlier. A very strict food plan at the beginning helped retrain my appetite.

I know what I will have for breakfast, since it's generally the same every morning: grapefruit juice, whole-grain cereal with milk, and decaffeinated coffee. I choose that menu because it's nutritious, quick and easy, and I like it. But my breakfast choice can be different. I occasionally have orange juice or fresh fruit, eggs, and whole wheat toast. Or, I might have fruit, cottage cheese, and toast.

Lunch is often a sandwich and fruit. The sandwich might be tuna salad, chicken salad, or Swiss cheese and turkey. The fruit is usually an apple or a banana. Or I might make a large salad or choose a hot entree and vegetables.

Dinner choices will include protein (probably fish), a complex carbohydrate (such as potatoes, brown rice, or pasta), vegetables, and possibly fruit or plain yogurt for dessert.

This is a general food plan I can live with. Minor variations in my plan are okay. If I'm invited to a friend's home, I eat moderate portions of what is served, but avoid sugar, alcohol, and caffeine, exactly as I do at home.

Keep Coming Back

What I must guard against is the temptation to snack before or after dinner. The food I eat at mealtime has never been the problem; what got me into deep trouble was nonstop snacking and eating for emotional reasons. My food plan is my salvation from the misery of compulsive eating.

Maintenance continues indefinitely. It's not always exciting, but it's infinitely more satisfactory than the binge-diet yo-yo. The goal is the same: to maintain abstinence and to work the program.

Progress, Not Perfection

If we could be perfect, we might find that finish line, the pot of gold at the end of the rainbow, but perfect we are not. Goodness knows, many of us tried hard enough. We wanted to look perfect, feel perfect, be perfect. Perfectionism was one of the characteristics that did us in. Our egos needed to be tamed for us to make a beginning with the program, to take the First Step of admitting "that we were powerless over food and our lives had become unmanageable."

The ego reduction continues as we move through the Steps. We become more sharply aware of our shortcomings, and we cultivate the humility that makes their removal possible. We learn to acknowledge mistakes, apologize, and make amends. We stop having to be right all of the time.

What a relief! It's okay to make mistakes! Not only is it okay, it's human. Regardless of how drastically we may have messed up our lives with compulsive eating, character defects, or whatever else, we are making progress toward recovery. We will continue to make mistakes; some of us will slide in and out of abstinence; all of us will have difficulties in our relationships with others. But we know more now than we did when we started the program. And we often grow by learning what not to do. Our program assures us there are no failures, only slow successes.

Progress for Ed K. means that he has found a new job after being fired for missing work and stealing food and money. Ed was bulimic. He has stopped purging, but has not yet had a binge-free month. But before he joined O.A., he was bingeing and purging four or five times a day. So Ed considers one or two binges a month to be fantastic progress. He reports, "I'm getting off the emotional merry-go-round of extreme highs and lows, and although I can't handle the idea of a God, I'm coming to believe in my group as a Higher Power. That's progress for me."

There is no finish line to emotional and spiritual growth. I hope that as long as I live I will be open to the grace that enables me to move away from self-will and become more like the person God intends me to be. I can work for a lifetime on coming closer to the ideal outlined in the Prayer of St. Francis of Assisi:

> Lord, make me a channel of thy peace—that where there is hatred I may bring love—that where there is wrong, I may bring the spirit of forgiveness—that where there is discord, I may bring harmony—that where there is error, I may bring truth—that where there is doubt, I may bring faith—that where there is despair, I may bring hope—that where there are shadows, I may bring light— that where there is sadness, I may bring joy. Lord, grant that I may seek rather to comfort than to be comforted— to understand, than to be understood—to love, than to be loved. For it is by self-forgetting that one finds. It is by forgiving that one is forgiven. It is by dying that one awakens to Eternal Life. Amen.[1]

I know that I will never reach this ideal. I probably will never have perfect abstinence either. By keeping the ideals in front of me, though, I stay on the right track—the path to inner peace and serenity.

A Daily Reprieve

So far, we have not found a magical cure for eating disorders. No vaccination provides permanent immunity against the craving to misuse food during times of stress or depression. We have not found a finish line, but we have found a program that promises us a daily reprieve from our illness if we remain spiritually fit and in tune with the God of our understanding.

Unlike alcohol and other drugs, food is not something we can remove from our lives and be done with. Food is necessary to sustain life, and we must come to terms with moderate consumption. A friend of mine in the program says he doesn't have a moderate bone in his body. I don't think I do either. That's why I have to get outside help.

When my Higher Power is at the center of my life, everything else, including food, falls into place. I need to make contact with my Higher Power each day, since, just as I must have food daily, I also need spiritual nourishment. My natural inclination is to overdo things I like and underdo things I don't like. I believe the progress I make in striking a more healthy balance is directly related to the time I spend improving my relationship with a Higher Power.

There is always more to learn and receive. It is fortunate, too, that opportunities for spiritual growth are not limited to the time we spend in prayer and meditation. Every daily experience can help us come closer to God's will. The key is stepping away from center stage and letting God direct the show.

I know a wonderful woman who says she owes her life to the Twelve Step program. Her name is Connie T., and she came to O.A. five years ago, weighing more than three hundred pounds. She had diabetes, dangerously high blood pressure, and very serious heart trouble. Since getting around was such a struggle for her, Connie had stopped going anywhere except to the grocery store and occasionally to church. Her husband had died, and she was completely alone except for two cats. Since she no longer kept in touch with former friends, her days revolved around her television set and refrigerator.

Five years ago, a woman in Connie's church persuaded her to go to an O.A. meeting. Connie said it wouldn't work; she branded the people at the meeting as "fanatics." She wouldn't have returned except that the place where the meetings were held, in her church, was across the street from where she lived, and she didn't have anything else to do on Wednesday evenings (or any other evening, for that matter).

"I dimly realized I craved human companionship," Connie says, "and I guess I had a tiny spark of hope. At first, I didn't speak to anyone at the meetings except my friend. What surprised me was that people spoke to me. I was used to feeling like a freak wherever I went, but I didn't feel that way at the meeting, even though I was by far the heaviest person there. Every time I went, for the first couple of months, I'd think that maybe the program might be okay for those other people, but it would never work for me. I'd decide not to go back.

"Then, when Wednesday rolled around again, a picture would pop into my mind of all of us standing in a circle, holding hands, saying the Lord's Prayer, and then saying, 'Keep coming back.' 'Keep coming back' would keep echoing through my head on Wednesday afternoons, and about six o'clock I'd decide to go back once more.

"I didn't get abstinent, but I felt better after a meeting. I rarely said anything. I'd just sit and listen and usually pass when my turn came. I didn't think anyone would want to hear about my problems. I didn't take any phone numbers either, but I'd write mine down in the book we passed around. When one of the women called me one afternoon, I was really surprised."

That phone call made the first dent in Connie's armor of isolation. "The next day I called her back, and I think that was the beginning of my recovery. I believe the phone call I got was my Higher Power's way of telling me I was okay just the way I was. I didn't have to hide because I weighed 328 pounds.

"I began talking more at meetings. A couple of other people called me. Then after about three months, a newcomer showed up who was almost as heavy as me, and she was a lot younger. After the meeting I talked to her. I told her I sure wasn't any authority on the program, but I knew how she felt, and we exchanged phone numbers."

Reaching out. Connie saw that someone else needed her help. From then on, she began to make progress with her own abstinence. "I really wanted to do something for Leslie. She has most of her life ahead of her. I was surprised at how concerned I was. It was as if God was showing me I could do something useful."

For the past four years, Connie has been taking newcomers under her wing and letting them know that someone cares. In the process, she has lost more than 100 pounds, and her physical health has greatly improved.

"It's a good day for me when I remember to be grateful for all I have," says Connie. "I'm grateful just to be alive! According to my doctor, that's something of a miracle. Five years ago, I didn't think I had anything to be alive for except maybe my cats. That's all changed, thanks to the program. I have so many friends now. Along with going to meetings, I'm working as a volunteer at a senior citizens' center, so I've got plenty to do.

"I'm convinced my Higher Power had some plans for me when He led me to the program. By all rights, I should be dead by now, but I'm not, and I believe there's a reason. It's up to me to find out what that reason is every day."

Connie has a daily reprieve from her illness, and so do you and I when we are spiritually alive and seeking to know and do God's will. We can only do that on a daily basis, since our Higher Power is always here in the present.

Keep Coming Back
We shall not cease from exploration
And the end of all our exploring
Will be to arrive where we started
And know the place for the first time.[2]

My first Twelve Step meeting consisted of five people in a

church basement twelve years ago. It was a simple, undramatic beginning to what has proven to be a quiet, continuing adventure. Through this adventure, my body, mind, heart, and spirit have changed and developed. They are becoming integrated in new ways. The more I explore and grow, the better I understand the wisdom presented to me at that first meeting, which I hear again every time I come back.

The Twelve Step wisdom is given to us over and over again, each time we come together to share our experiences, strengths, and hopes. We never learn all there is to learn, and we never fully "practice the principles in all our affairs." That's why we keep coming back.

We tried to find a magic "fix" for the pain, disappointment, and frustration of living. For a while, food seemed to work the magic. When we became compulsive about food and obsessed with it, we looked for another magic fix. But nothing we tried worked for long. Sooner or later, we concluded that no magic fix will kill the pain that is an inevitable part of being alive.

There is no way to avoid our share of disappointment and frustration. If we try to escape into food, or drugs, or unhealthy behavior, the pain of addiction can grow much worse than the pain we thought we could avoid. Although we can't escape the painful part of living, we can learn how to deal with it. We don't have to do it alone. There is help. We can help each other.

In learning to cope with our weaknesses through the Twelve Steps, we discover how our weaknesses may be turned into strengths. Because we finally accept our lack of power, the limits of self-will, we are able to tap into a source of strength greater than our own, beyond ourselves: a Higher Power. That's what makes us grateful to be recovering—we're probably stronger now than we would have been without our illness.

The message I'd like to leave with you is simple: Don't give up. No matter how many problems you may be having with abstinence and the Steps, keep coming back. The problems outside the program are worse than those inside. No one of us works this program perfectly. All we need to do is continue to give it our best shot.

The longer we stay around the meeting rooms, the better our chances are of catching the new life. As the truth of the program filters through our experience, insight comes, and so does understanding. Insight and understanding translate into action. What may seem naive, simplistic, or unbelievable at first takes on firm credibility as we see positive changes occurring in the lives of real people.

I first believed abstinence was possible when I saw and heard people who were practicing it. So, too, with the Steps and principles of the program—I came to believe they worked because I saw real results. If I had stayed in my kitchen with the company of my refrigerator, I would never have known the amazingly rich experiences of the past twelve years. There have been and will continue to be ups and downs. That's life without a fairy godmother. The advantage is that it's real life instead of a fantasy.

Keep coming back!

THE TWELVE STEPS OF OVEREATERS ANONYMOUS

1. We admitted we were powerless over food—that our lives had become unmanageable.

2. Came to believe that a Power greater than ourselves could restore us to sanity.

3. Made a decision to turn our will and our lives over to the care of God *as we understood Him.*

4. Made a searching and fearless moral inventory of ourselves.

5. Admitted to God, to ourselves, and to another human being the exact nature of our wrongs.

6. Were entirely ready to have God remove all these defects of character.

7. Humbly asked him to remove our shortcomings.

8. Made a list of all persons we had harmed, and became willing to make amends to them all.

9. Made direct amends to such people wherever possible, except when to do so would injure them or others.

10. Continued to take personal inventory and when we were wrong promptly admitted it.

11. Sought through prayer and meditation to improve our conscious contact with God *as we understood him,* praying only for knowledge of His will for us and the power to carry that out.

12. Having had a spiritual awakening as the result of these steps, we tried to carry this message to compulsive over-eaters and to practice these principles in all our affairs.*

---

*Adapted from the Twelve Steps of Alcoholics Anonymous, reprinted with permission of A.A. World Services, Inc., New York, N.Y.

THE TWELVE STEPS OF ALCOHOLICS ANONYMOUS

1. We admitted we were powerless over alcohol—that our lives had become unmanageable.

2. Came to believe that a Power greater than ourselves could restore us to sanity.

3. Made a decision to turn our will and our lives over to the care of God *as we understood him.*

4. Made a searching and fearless moral inventory of ourselves.

5. Admitted to God, to ourselves, and to another human being the exact nature of our wrongs.

6. Were entirely ready to have God remove all these defects of character.

7. Humbly asked him to remove our shortcomings.

8. Made a list of all persons we had harmed, and became willing to make amends to them all.

9. Made direct amends to such people wherever possible, except when to do so would injure them or others.

10. Continued to take personal inventory and when we were wrong promptly admitted it.

11. Sought through prayer and meditation to improve our conscious contact with God *as we understood him,* praying only for knowledge of His will for us and the power to carry that out.

12. Having had a spiritual awakening as the result of these steps, we tried to carry this message to alcoholics, and to practice these principles in all our affairs.*

---

*The Twelve Steps are taken from *Alcoholics Anonymous* (Third Edition), published by A.A. World Services, Inc., New York, NY, pp. 59-60. Reprinted with permission.

ENDNOTES

Chapter Four

1. *Twenty-four Hours a Day,* Revised Edition (Center City, MN: Hazelden Educational Materials, 1975), entry for January 11.

Chapter Six

1. Dag Hammarskjold, *Markings* (New York: Alfred A. Knopf, 1964), 8.

2. Steven Levenkron, *The Best Little Girl in the World* (New York: Warner Books, 1979).

Chapter Nine

1. Dylan Thomas, *The Collected Poems of Dylan Thomas* (New York: New Directions Books, James Laughlin, 1939), 128.

Chapter Ten

1. Robert Louis Stevenson, *A Child's Garden of Verses* (New York: Delacorte Press, 1985), 42.

2. *For Today* (Torrance, CA: Overeaters Anonymous, Inc., 1982), 293.

Chapter Eleven

1. *Alcoholics Anonymous* (New York: Alcoholics Anonymous World Services, Inc., 1955), 83-84.

Chapter Twelve

1. *Twelve Steps and Twelve Traditions* (New York: Alcoholics Anonymous World Services, Inc., 1952), 102.

2. T. S. Eliot, *Collected Poems. 1909-1962* (London: Faber and Faber Limited, 1974), 222.

INDEX

Abstinence:
  adventure of, 7-10;
  as a spiritual journey, 12-15;
  as an invitation to intimacy, 10-12;
  expectations in, 95;
  long-term, 46-47;
  meaning of, 8, 40;
  preconceptions of, 5;
  progress toward, 38-41;
  relative to spiritual condition, 47
Adolescence:
  relationship to food in, 10, 59-60
Al-Anon, 29, 85
Alcohol:
  danger to abstinence, 9, 23, 50, 59, 114
Alcoholics Anonymous, 29, 43, 48, 56, 86
Alcoholics Anonymous, 105
Anorexia, 36

Bingeing, 26, 37-38, 40, 43, 73-74
Body types, 40
Bottoming out, 51-53
Bulimia, 36

Christian Science Monitor, 22
Communication, 29-30, 49
Cultural pressure, 6, 37, 57-58